Origin of Yoga &
Pashupata Yoga

With kind regards, ॐ and prem

Origin of Yoga & Pashupata Yoga

Swami Niranjanananda Saraswati

Discourses from the Yogadrishti (Yogavision) series of satsangs at Ganga Darshan Vishwa Yogapeeth and Baidyanatheshwar Shankarbagh (Shivalaya), Munger, in January and February 2010

Yoga Publications Trust, Munger, Bihar, India

Published by Yoga Publications Trust
First edition 2011

ISBN: 978-81-86336-97-7

Publisher and distributor: Yoga Publications Trust, Ganga Darshan, Munger, Bihar, India.

Website: www.biharyoga.net
www.rikhiapeeth.net

Printed at Aegean Offset Printers, Greater Noida

Dedication

To our guru Sri Swami Satyananda Saraswati
who continues to inspire and guide us
on our spiritual journey.

Contents

Prologue

In March 2009, before departing for a program in Australia, I had visited our guru, Sri Swami Satyananda, to ask for his blessings. On that occasion, he told me that this would be my last travel for a program overseas, as my *parivrajaka*, wandering life, was coming to an end. A few months later, in July, he gave a clear indication of what I had to accomplish in the next phase of my life and gave a comprehensive plan for the next twenty years. He said, "From 2010, your gradual introduction to the new phase of life has to begin. Remaining steady in one place, focus on sadhana, swadhyaya, satsang and sannyasa." He also said, "Don't give up yoga. Continue to work for the development of yoga alongside the other direction that you are required to walk in. In the process of developing yoga, give satsangs on every subject of yoga."

The way yoga is commonly perceived or understood is not a complete picture of yoga. People know yoga as its different branches: hatha yoga, raja yoga, karma yoga, kriya yoga or bhakti yoga. Did these branches develop independently over a course of time? Are they each capable of taking an individual to the ultimate aim of human life? Or are they all part of a greater design for human evolution, and complementary to each other? From our perspective, they are not independent subjects developed by different people over time.

If one studies the scriptures and literatures handed down by the forerunners of the yogic tradition, one finds that they always gave a complete picture or plan of yoga before specifically focusing on a technique or practice, whether it be Rishi Vasishtha, Adi Shankaracharya, Sri Krishna, or other sages who came later. This indicates that all the different practices of yoga are part of a bigger picture which is not known to the ordinary human being. Even if people come across these teachings, they do not grasp them due to the popular approach they are conditioned to. Therefore, they continue to focus on the individual branches of hatha yoga, raja yoga, jnana yoga, kundalini yoga or kriya yoga and a true perspective of yoga is never acquired.

To comprehend yoga as it was originally perceived and taught, one needs to develop an understanding of its classical roots as well as the practical application of its various aspects. As the understanding becomes deeper and subtler, fresh insights are gained, the subjects evolve spontaneously and become a living experience. One is able to perceive the stream running through the different branches of yoga and arrive at the point where this stream merges with the sea.

1

The Original Question

The story of yoga, the journey through the history of yoga, began thousands of years ago when people used to live in tribes in forests and jungles. The idea of hamlets where small collections of people came together and lived was possibly only a recent. At that time, in the middle of a deep forest lived an ascetic. The ascetic was renowned in the community, in that sparsely populated human society, as a person of great attainments and high realizations. In those days it was permitted for ascetics to live a family life, and this ascetic was also married.

One day, he was sitting with his wife, his consort and disciple, and she asked him a question: "We live in idyllic surroundings, everything is provided for. Nature has given plenty of game all around, streams of pure water, trees laden with fruit, farms filled with grains. There is prosperity everywhere. However, people do not identify with the prosperity; they identify with suffering. They seek pleasure and happiness, and their life passes in a quest for little things which will please their mind. The time passes trying to avoid suffering and pain, and nobody is able to be free of the suffering. It seems that this is the law, this is the nature of creation. Is there a way by which one can overcome the pain and suffering, and attain eternal peace, contentment and fulfilment?"

After listening to this question, the ascetic answered: "Yes, there are ways by which one can overcome the suffering and pain in life. However, in order to do so, the aim, purpose and direction in life has to be clear. Life must have a goal; it must have a focus which is not merely enjoyment. We are not born to only enjoy the fleeting years in search of moments which bring happiness and contentment. Life must have a focus, there has to be a reason for living beyond the material reality."

She now asked: "Is there a predetermined focus in life, or are human beings free to have their own goal and focus?"

The ascetic answered: "The goal of every manifest life form is predetermined, just as nature is predetermined. How far they will go in their life is predetermined. How long they will live is predetermined, the number of times the breath will be inhaled and exhaled is predetermined, as is the number of times the heart will beat. Nobody will be able to take an extra breath after their predetermined last breath. There is a predetermined destiny for everything and the same applies to human life. If one wants to create one's own destiny or make a new destiny, then the attempt which such aspirants, students or seekers need to make is to tune in to aid their predestined direction, to walk the predestined direction and not struggle against it."

She asked further: "What is the goal of life? Is there somebody who controls us, or are we free and independent units? We enjoy the world while we live. We die and take birth again, and continue the process of seeking pleasure and enjoyment and avoiding suffering."

The ascetic answered: "The goal of life is predetermined and it is the predetermined nature that manifests in all life forms. A mango will not become a banana and a banana will not become a strawberry. In the same manner, the nature and destiny of a human being will not change. The predestined human nature will carry the human being forward until their destiny is accomplished. However, nature has locked away the knowledge of that destiny. Nobody can know what is destined for them."

She asked: "Why is it unknown to people? If it is predetermined, why is it unknown?"

4

The ascetic answered: "If they know what is predestined, they will not strive to make any effort, they will not try to improve the quality of their life. They will stagnate in whatever stage and condition they are in. Thus it is also predestined that the predestined nature, behaviour and karmas will remain unknown to the person who is living them out. The person only becomes a tool through which destiny plays its role."

She asked: "Can you explain this in a different way? What is our nature? How do we live our life in this world, and how can we find eternal satisfaction and overcome suffering and pain in life?"

The ascetic now began a series of discourses in which he explained to his consort and disciple the nature of the universe, life, divinity, the transcendental nature, the causes of identification and bondage in life and the means to overcome them and become free to experience liberation.

5

The consort, the questioner and student, was Parvati. The ascetic was Shiva. The yogic process which Shiva described to Parvati is influenced by tantra. That is why yoga has been described as an offshoot of tantra. In the original instructions of yoga, it was Shiva who narrated the systems, disciplines, philosophy and theory of yoga to Parvati. Shiva was also the founder of the tantras. Therefore, the yogic concepts propounded by Shiva are influenced by tantric theories.

Pashupata yoga

The first yoga propounded by Shiva was known as Pashupata yoga. Not hatha yoga, not raja yoga, not kundalini yoga, not karma yoga, not bhakti yoga. The name was Pashupata yoga. This original name of yoga describes the aim of yoga. *Pashu* means animal and *pati* means master. Therefore, it is the yoga in which one becomes aware of the relationship that exists between one's self and the divine in the form of slave and master.

There are three concepts. One, the pati or the master. God Almighty is the master. Two, *pashu* or the animal. Individual beings are animals. We are animals. The level of our performance and existence is more instinctive and less rational. Therefore, individual life forms are *pashus*. Three, the tool with which the master controls the animals, which is a *pasha*, which means noose, leash or chain. How does one control a wild animal? How does one control an untrained dog? By putting a chain around its neck. How does one control a wild horse? By putting a rope around its neck. How does one control a wild camel, elephant or tiger? By putting a noose around its neck. That is a pasha, the controlling agent through which the master can control animals.

The cause of the unrestrained, dissipated and aggressive behaviour of all is *malas* and *vikaras,* impurities of nature. The leash, without which the animals would be violent, aggressive and run directionless, is the leash of different disciplines. One needs to acquire different disciplines in life to remain controlled and restrained.

6

The understanding of yoga evolves with these concepts of tantra. They form the foundation or basis of Pashupata yoga, the yoga in which a relationship is defined between the controller: the master, and the animal: the individual.

Pati and pashu

Pati indicates a power, a being that is able to control the lower manifestations, lower behaviours and existences. It controls all life forms and indicates the existence of a power or entity which is the cause of every life form. That entity is called spirit. People believe in the existence of spirit even though they have not seen it and cannot define it. Without direct experience or cognition, the concept of spirit is accepted as real. This conditioning, this level of belief in and identification with something one has never seen, is the pati nature in every pashu.

The pashu is a conditioned animal who acts within defined parameters. It is not free to act freely; it has to act within the defined parameters of its ego, intellect, beliefs, level of mental evolution, norms of society, and personal beliefs of right and wrong. The pashu is bound by all such factors. It is a conditioned being and must live within the confines of its conditionings.

An example: people often fall prey to their ego initiatives, whether in a positive or a negative way. They find fault with everyone except themselves. They blame the whole world for their agony, frustrations and tensions, and never want to change themselves. The negativity is always projected on to other people and they are always justified, always right. However, this is only an ego manifestation; it is not the reality. This is the conditioned nature of the pashu. In the guise of morality, justice and dharma, many such ego expressions are played out, and one doesn't even know that this is what is going on. Such situations represent the inability to confront one's weaknesses. This is the conditioned nature of the pashu, while pati, the master, is unconditioned. He is not bound by any defined parameters of ego, intellect, senses, belief or ideology. The free state of existence is the pati state. Pati is the cosmic spirit: free, eternal, infinite, which is the witness of all, while the bound, contained or restrained state of existence is the pashu state.

Pashu is the *jiva*, the individual. Why has the individual spirit been called pashu? The scriptures say that there are 84,000 *yonis*, species, and the spirit has to go through all these states before it can acquire a human birth. It evolves by undergoing the experiences of these life forms and finally acquires the state of a human being.

There is only one speciality of the human form and that is what differentiates it from an animal. A human being possesses intellect. A dog feels hungry, but it is not aware that it is hungry. If a man feels hungry, he knows that he is hungry. Among the 84,000 species that exist, only humankind possesses intellect, knowledge, awareness. If this faculty is removed, a human being is as good as an animal.

Unfortunately, human beings do not use this gift of know-ledge properly; instead, they misuse it. Duryodhana says in the *Mahabharata*: *Jaanaami dharmam na cha me pravrittih; jaanaami adharmam na cha me nivrittih* – "I know what is righteous, but I feel no interest or attraction towards it; I know what is unrighteous, but I cannot free myself of it." This means that even if one possesses knowledge, one is still steeped in ignorance; one is not able to use one's knowledge appropriately. That is why human beings have not been able to attain their humanity.

Those who have been able to use their knowledge appropriately have attained humanity. They are the siddhas, rishis, munis, renunciates and saints. They made knowledge the base to take their life on the path of growth and evolution, and were able to evolve. However, when knowledge is not used properly, narrow and negative actions and behaviour manifest, and gain prominence in life. Once this happens, life is ruined. That is when the individual has a downfall; one falls down the well of darkness and is not able to come out of it. Such a being has been called pashu: one who is trapped in the bondage of *prakriti*, nature.

Becoming the master

The focus of life must be for every pashu to realize that it has the potential and the inherent ability to become a pati. Every individual must realize that they can become the master, the controller. That is the *purushartha*, effort, and focus of the pashu: to transform from being a slave to instinctive living to being the controller, free from the conditions which restrict and inhibit the expression of life.

The conditions which bind one to this plane have to lessen. The desires which bind one to this plane have to lessen. The expectations that give birth to different cravings, moods and conditions of the mind have to lessen. A greater quietude of consciousness has to be instilled. The way to attain this is sadhana.

Sadhana is the process by which the pashu can become pati. That is the meaning of the name of the first yoga, Pashupata tantra or Pashupata yoga.

The attachments and attractions to sense objects create different conditions of the mind. If two different colours are combined, they will give birth to a third colour. In the same manner, when a sense object, which is external, combines with one's internal awareness of that sense object, it gives birth to a third condition in the mind, which is desire.

Imagine that you come into a room without knowledge of what the room contains. As your eyes go around the room, you see a beautiful, unique golden flower in full bloom. That object is separate from you, but by entering the room and observing it, you suddenly become aware of it. By becoming aware of it, you have many different thoughts quickly about its beauty, grace and nature, and suddenly a desire forms in your mind: "I wish I could have it."

An external object and a personal awareness give birth to a third factor: desire. This desire then gives birth to action, which can help fulfil the desire. The chain goes on. This is what must be reduced, as an increase in desire means an increase in *vrittis*, patterns of the mind. A decrease in desire means a decrease in vrittis. Therefore, the disciplines and

9

systems that evolved in Pashupata tantra guide an individual to realize the journey from being a pashu to becoming the pati, by following a process and system which helps restrain the inner dissipations and provides greater focus to understand, manage, work with and transform the effects of the interaction with the world that one goes through in life.

Shiva explained to his first disciple, his consort, that in this conditioned life exists the possibility to experience the unconditioned existence. In order to experience that unconditioned existence, one must realize how one interacts with the world, with the *moola vrittis* and *vikshepas*, the conditionings and distractions, and by which method, *vidhi*, one can come to a state of balance in life and thus eradicate suffering and pain and experience happiness. This is how the concept of yoga originated.

2

Understanding Suffering

The original philosophy of yoga as expounded by the ascetic Shiva to his disciple and consort Parvati came about with the question that Parvati asked, "How can one overcome pain and suffering in life?" To this Shiva answered, "Suffering is not necessarily pain, but a change in the static existence of life." You can observe this in your own life. When you are not able to handle change, it is experienced as suffering, but if you are comfortable with change, it does not become suffering.

Source of suffering
The suffering or the disturbance that is experienced in the static state has three sources. One category of suffering is caused by natural calamities, and is called *adhidaivic*. Global warming is a cause of suffering. The external climate creates suffering. It disturbs the ease of the body, mind and prana. Disturbance in the ease of life is known as suffering. Suffering does not necessitate that one screams and cries and asks for solace; it is disturbance in the natural ease and comfort of life, which changes the mental behaviour and emotional makeup. It changes everything.

If the weather turns cold, the body begins to shiver. The natural ease of the body is disturbed and that is felt as suffering. If sufficient warm clothes are worn, the cold still exists but one does not perceive it as suffering. The same is true of heat or any other natural circumstance. If one is unable to

11

adjust to it, it becomes the cause of suffering and disturbance. If one is able to adjust to it, there is no suffering.

The second source of suffering is *adhyatmic*, destined, unknown, emanating from within in the form of samskaras and karmas, or *swabhava*, the nature of an individual. If the karmas and nature of an individual are tamasic, their life will be tamasic. If the nature and character of an individual is rajasic, their life will be rajasic. If they are sattwic, their life will be sattwic. The karmas, samskaras, gunas and nature that one comes endowed with are a cause of disturbance in the ease of life, for one is not able to control, channel or even realize the inner unconscious behaviours.

The third source of suffering, called *adhibhautic*, is identification or interaction with one's surroundings. This is the main source of suffering and pain in human life. People always try to justify their association with things that have no relevance in their life. For years they remain attached to events, people or circumstances that have influenced and affected their life, whether positively or negatively, and continue to carry the old baggage.

Somebody may have rebuked you ten or twenty years ago, but the memory of that rebuke is still fresh in the mind. The stress created by that rebuke is still fresh in the mind, and when you come across the person with whom you had the altercation, you remember that particular moment which turned you against him or him against you. You remember the moment of crisis, the moment when your personal case and comfort was disturbed. This happens all the time.

In the ashram, one learns to recognize one's altercations as ego clashes: your ego clashing with someone else's ego. That ego clash is suffering. It takes one away from the state of peace and bliss, and induces a state of disturbance and anxiety. That is weakness of the ego. When the ego is weak, it becomes arrogant. There is a saying, "Inside every bully, there is a crying child waiting to come out." When the ego is weak, it develops a hard character. If the ego is strong, it becomes soft, as you are confident and do not worry about

anything. You are only concerned with maintaining a clear mind. With a weak ego, you put a lot of rubbish in the mind and try to hide behind different masks. That is suffering, due to stress, ego, personal expectations and associations.

Effect of maya

Suffering is thus defined in several ways by the tantric tradition: an expression of the ego, the result of interaction with sense objects, the influence of the external natural environment, or a quirk of personality in the form of karmas and samskaras. Anyone who is born into this life and becomes a life member of this planet is subject to suffering or change. However, that is not the problem. The problem is the inability to adjust to change, due to the association with the senses and sense objects. This is known as maya.

There is a story that Maya and Bhakti were sisters. Maya used to wear torn and old clothes while Bhakti would wear bright and beautiful clothes. The two used to live together. That was the time when everyone was attracted to Bhakti, as she was beautiful and always wore beautiful clothes and ornaments. People would be repelled by Maya, as she seemed poor and did not possess beauty or dress attractively. Watching how people were always attracted to Bhakti, Maya became jealous of her. She wondered how she could take Bhakti's place so people would notice her. One morning, when the two sisters went to bathe in the pond, Maya finished her bath quickly, got out of the pond, wore Bhakti's clothes and walked away. When Bhakti emerged, she found that her clothes were gone and she was left with Maya's dirty and torn clothes, and she was forced to wear them.

From that day onwards, people have chased Maya and not Bhakti. Maya has become glamorous and Bhakti appears simple. This is the mentality that everyone possesses today.

Once caught by Maya, only pain is experienced. Maya makes you chase her; she catches you by the noose of sense objects. Maya deludes the *jiva*, the individual; she takes the jiva's mind away from God to sense objects. She says: "Look! How nice this world is. It has riches and glamour; it has the pleasures of taste, sight, smell and touch. The body, mind and emotions will experience pleasure in these, so enjoy them." Once caught in this trap of maya, one experiences suffering. It is the *pasha*, noose, of maya that keeps the jiva in bondage, that keeps one in the pashu state.

Maya means illusion, a momentary exposure or glimpse, a fleeting thing before something else comes in the range of one's awareness. Maya is the cause of the distraction of consciousness. It is because of maya that suffering is natural to life and it is also because of maya that people don't want to expose themselves to suffering. It is because of maya that people believe that their body can remain dry while diving in the ocean. Everyone believes that 'I am part of this world, but I am a unique and independent individual in the world.' Everybody dives into the ocean, but wishes their body would remain dry. That is not possible.

If you dive into the ocean, your body is bound to get wet. The water will surround you from all sides. In the same way, when you come into this world, maya surrounds you from all sides in the form of *avidya*, ignorance. You think you know, but you don't. Avidya is the first armour or clothing of the individual spirit. It is the first covering on the free and liberated state of the individual spirit, the one who is interacting in the world, living in the world, experiencing the change and suffering in the world. It is because of avidya that one is unable to adjust to change. It is because of avidya, the first covering on the luminosity of the spirit, that the radiance of the spirit is diminished.

If a piece of coloured paper is placed over a light bulb, the intensity of the clear light will diminish. The light will seem less intense in colour. The more coverings there are, the less luminosity there will be. Ultimately, when too many layers have been put, the light will not shine through at all. In the same manner, the spirit is luminous, but in this world and life, it is subject to maya. Maya is part of identification; you identify with something in search of happiness and pleasure, in the hope that you will be fulfilled by the identification. That is maya, and maya or avidya makes you lose your personal awareness. Personal awareness means 'Who am I? Am I this bulb? Am I this Individual? Or am I the free, transcendental nature?'

Everything has an essence, which must be understood. Mud is taken from the ground and made into a pot. When it becomes a pot, it adopts a new form, quality and name. It is not mud lying on the ground any more. However, the essence, the basic quality, is mud. After the pot is destroyed, it again reverts to earth and becomes mud. In the same manner, the luminosity of the spirit is eternal, but it takes a form in this life, an identity, and that form or identity becomes you and me. Just as one covers the body with clothes, the spirit is covered by different layers of maya, of knowing and not knowing, which give it a distinct and definite experience in life. That experience, until it is understood and used as a stepping stone to evolution, growth and progress, is felt as bondage and suffering.

Nature of samsara and jiva

When one is born into this life, the mind and consciousness experience bondage. The attractions in life divert the attention from the self-contained and pure awareness to a dis-

15

sipated and distracted awareness. When this dissipated and distracted awareness attaches itself to different sense objects, it creates a desire to own them, possess them, experience them, and to find that moment of happiness by acquiring, realizing, knowing or using them. This is how identification with the outside world of the senses begins. As one begins to recognize things around oneself, one becomes alienated from the inner state of peace, contentment and silence, and gives way to desires, needs, expectations and ambitions.

The individual entity or person who is the pashu, the conditioned being, is a diverted and distracted being, who is totally mesmerized by sense objects and the sensorial world. For the fleeting period of time that is called a lifetime, the only need is fulfilment of sensorial desires: somebody to pat you on the back, somebody to pat you on the mind, somebody to pat you on the emotions and somebody to pat you on the spirit. With four pats you are happy. When somebody pats you on the back, of course you feel happy. When somebody pats you on the mind, you feel elated. When somebody pats you on your emotions, you feel on top of the world. And when somebody pats you spiritually, you feel that you are the master! Different behaviours manifest with different pats. However, all these pats make you dependent on something external for experiencing happiness.

It is said that every desire is impregnated with another desire before it even takes birth, before the first one actualizes. One attention, one awareness, one identification is enough to create one desire, and that desire is enough to create a chain of events which will bind one to that object for a long time. This is how the human mind in this world becomes distracted and diverted, and the pashu nature becomes even more defined. The aggressive, hard-willed, self-oriented expectations and desires become more defined in life. As these natures become more defined, they are identified as tamasic. As they become less defined, they are identified as sattwic. If something is defined one hundred percent, it is tamasic. If something is defined ten percent, it is on the sattwic side.

16

The conditioned behaviour is a response to one's interaction with the world of senses and sense objects. The senses are interacting with the world, the mind is interacting with the world, the emotions are interacting with the world, the spirit is experiencing the world. All this makes one more conditioned, ingrained, identified and absorbed, more a pashu.

Shiva explains to Parvati that the nature of the world is sorrow and misery because the world is created by *prakriti*, nature. The nature of prakriti is manifestation and externalization. The world is a place where the mind, consciousness and senses of a human being are always extroverted. Whoever is born in this world is entrapped by the influence of the senses, the fourfold aspects of the mind and objects.

It is the nature of the senses to be extroverted. If the senses become introverted, the world will not be able to function properly. If the *antahkarana*, inner instrument, becomes quiet, one will not be able to connect with the world. The scriptures mention that a human being has five *karmendriyas*, organs of actions, five *jnanendriyas*, organs of cognition, and

the fourfold mind, antahkarana or *manah chatushtaya*, comprised of *manas*, rationality, *buddhi*, intellect, *chitta*, memory, and *ahamkara*, ego, and their nature is to be extroverted. In the *Bhagavad Gita*, Sri Krishna says to Arjuna (15:7):

Mamaivaansho jeevaloke jeeva bhootah sanatanah;
Manah shashthaani indriyaani prakritisthaani karshati.

It is a part of me that becomes attracted by Prakriti, and through this attraction enters the realm of Prakriti, the manifest world. When it is born in the world, it is equipped with six sense organs, including the mind.

It is through the six sense organs that one becomes aware of life and the world, as it is their natural propensity to be attached to the world. When one becomes attached to the world, one is influenced by two conditions of the world: *raga* and *dwesha*, attraction and repulsion. Raga gives birth to pleasure and dwesha gives birth to pain. It is said in the *Yoga Sutras* (1:14):

Sukhah anushayi ragah; dukhah anushayi dweshah.

There is attraction for the pleasurable; there is repulsion from that which brings suffering.

Pleasure and pain are equal. If one is attracted towards something, it is due to a desire for pleasure. Attraction and attachment are born from pleasure. On the other hand, one feels detached and repelled by pain, and wants to run away from it. These are the two circumstances, pleasure and pain, from which raga and dwesha are born. They influence the fourfold mind and the senses, through which one lives in the world. Thus, suffering and joy go hand in hand in this world.

Search for happiness

The spirit is always trying to break free of suffering, of maya, and find its essence. After all, why is one drawn to spirituality? Not just to acquire knowledge, but to attain peace and happiness. This search has been perennial. From ancient times till today, people have searched for peace and happiness. Everyone aspires for them but they don't find them, as they don't know the way. This is because neither the nature of the individual being nor the world is conditioned for peace and happiness.

There is a story in the scriptures. Once there was a king. For many years he enjoyed the privileges of kingship, but all along he wanted to experience peace, contentment and happiness. He never found them, as throughout his reign, he faced stress, anxiety and wars. He became old, and decided to hand over the kingdom to his son and depart for the forests to live a life of contemplation, with the hope and thought that now in solitude he would try to understand the nature of the world and life. Thus he began to spend his time in contemplation, meditation, worship and prayer. Yet, he was not able to find the answer to his question: what is the real nature of the world?

One day, he had finished his prayers and was sitting outside his hut immersed in thought. An old man arrived before him and asked, "What are you doing in this forest? Who are you? Where have you come from?" The king offered the old man a seat, gave him food and then told his story. "Once I was a king and for years I enjoyed all the pleasures of my position, but I never found peace, joy or contentment. From the very beginning I wanted to know the nature of this world and life. Finally, I have handed over the throne to my son and come to the forest to live a life of contemplation." The old man said, "Come with me. We will go for a walk."

The old man took the king to the deeper part of the forest and they kept on walking. Eventually, the king was tired and wanted to rest. The old man led him to a tree which had no leaves, flowers or fruit, only thorns, and said, "Rest under this tree." The king found this strange. Nevertheless, he sat down. A soft breeze was blowing and he became drowsy. As soon as the king closed his eyes, the old man began to shake the tree and all the dry thorns started to fall and prick the king. He woke with a start and angrily shouted at the old man, "What are you doing? First you make me rest under a thorny tree, and when I try to rest you begin to shake it!" The old man started laughing. He said, "My king, I brought you here for a special purpose – to explain to you the nature of the world." The king said, "What do you mean?" The old man said, "The world is like this tree. It does not have leaves, flowers or fruit. It is only laden with thorns. Every living being spends their life under this thorny tree. When the wind blows and the thorns begin to fall, you call it suffering. When the wind stops for some time and the thorns do not fall and prick, you call it joy. Joy is experienced only momentarily, whereas pain is the eternal companion in this world. This is the nature of the world. No matter what you do, you cannot find joy here without pain accompanying it. Joy is transitory, not eternal."

The king said, "You have explained the nature of the world. Now tell me what the purpose of life is." The old man said, "O king, you ruled over a kingdom for seventy years. What was the purpose of your life then?" The king replied, "I had only one purpose: attaining joy, peace and prosperity." The old man said, "That is the purpose and reason for life. Every human being wants to experience joy, peace and prosperity. Only when you acquire them does the inner agitation come to an end. That is when the mind becomes still and you can make the effort for spiritual evolution."

The rungs of creation

The nature of the world, with its pain and joy, is an inherent aspect of its place in the rung of creation, as the process of creation is a step-down process from the transcendental realm to the conditioned realm.

State of potentiality: Before creation came into being, there was nothing. There was no manifestation, *tattwas* or elements. There was void, total darkness.

In that eternal void, a flame manifests. A flame is a form of light, and it has been said in the Samkhya philosophy that the nature of sattwa is light, luminosity. Thus, luminosity manifests in that deep darkness in the form of a flame. In that luminosity, all the *gunas*, qualities of nature, are in a state of balance, for pure sattwa holds rajas and tamas in perfect balance. That state has been called *Krishna* or *avyakta*. The word *krishna* means that which is hidden in darkness. God remains hidden in the heart; Krishna remains hidden in the heart. He remains hidden in the cave of the heart and no one can see him. In the unmanifest state, there is a tattwa, element, that remains hidden and cannot be experienced. That element has been called Krishna: that which is hidden in darkness, but is complete in itself.

The first manifestation of the supreme element is in the form of a flame, which is pure consciousness. That is the fundamental state of potentiality. The Krishna or avyakta state is like the state of a seed. If you hold the seed of a mango tree in your hand, you will not be able to see the tree in it, but the potential to become a tree is hidden in that seed. It can become a huge tree; it can assume the form of leaves, flowers and fruit. This means that all possibilities are inherent in it. The seed and tree are not different from each other. In the same way, in that supreme, conscious flame, all the elements of *srishti*, creation, *palan*, maintenance, and *samhara*, destruction, exist in a state of balance.

Basis of creation: When that conscious flame shoots forth and assumes different forms, its first task is to create a foundation for creation, maintenance and destruction. Thus it has been said that the first expression of the avyakta state is in the form of the three gunas: *sattwa*, luminosity; *rajas*, dynamism; *tamas*, stagnation. Sattwa guna is indicated by *prakasha*, luminosity, rajo guna is indicated by *kriyasheelata*, dynamism, and tamo guna is indicated by *sthiti*, assumption of a conditioned state in which there is no change.

After the gunas, there is manifestation of mahat, ahamkara, tanmatras, the senses: sound, taste, form, touch, smell, etc. This becomes the basis of creation.

The conditioned state: In the sequence of creation, when the individual spirit comes into a body, it acquires a state which

21

is conditioned and limited. This is due to the predominance of tamo guna in this state. When a statue is formed out of a stone which did not have any defined shape or form, the stone acquires a form. It comes into a conditioned state. That is tamo guna.

By coming into a body, the individual spirit has assumed a form, *akara*, and lives according to that form. The first aspect of this conditioned state is *ahamkara*: aham+akara, 'my form', awareness of 'me'. The moment a form is assumed, limitedness is experienced. Where there is limitedness, there is pain, sorrow and stress, as the spirit wants to be free; it does not want to remain bound. Ahamkara is the first form that the consciousness assumes, and that makes it engage in the objects of the world. If 'akara' was removed from ahamkara, only 'aham' would remain, and in that I-ness without form there is awareness of God: *Aham Brahmasmi* – "I am That Element and there is no difference between the two." There is awareness of *Tat Twam Asi*: "You are That." Right now, one cannot say "I am That", as one is defined by the awareness of form, but once awareness of the form is removed, one would be able to say "I am That." That is called *mukti*, *moksha*, becoming free from the bondage of karmas. It has been said:

Jala mein kumbha, kumbha mein jala, baahara bheetara paani;
Phootahi kumbha, jala jalahi samaanaa, baata kahiye jnani.

Pot in the water, water in the pot, water out and in;
Pot breaks, water merges with water, this the wise explain.

When the individual spirit finds itself in a limited state, it experiences pain. However, once the pot breaks, the water of the pot becomes one with the water of the ocean. Once the form disappears, the self which is one with the Supreme Self is experienced and there is no more suffering.

22

3

Effort and Grace

There needs to be an effort, a sankalpa, to change one's life, to remove the defects and shortcomings and bring in excellence. Once excellence comes into life, once life is infused with positive qualities, positive thoughts, actions and behaviour, one becomes the recipient of God's grace.

Sri Swamiji says that people go to gurus, temples and religious places in the hope of finding grace. People pray to God, "God, please remove my suffering." They pray and come back and don't find the grace, as nobody is willing to

change their life. They expect miracles in life. Let me tell you clearly today: nothing is achieved by praying unless you make the effort to bring a change into your life. Until you bring about a change in your behaviour, actions and thinking, do not expect to receive God's grace, for God helps those who help themselves. He supports those who are eager to improve their lives. Those who do not want to change their lives can go and pray every day, but God will say, "What is the point? You want a miracle in your life, but you do not want to change your life. You do not want to change your thinking, your samskaras, your actions, your behaviour, so what will you do with my blessings? Even if a miracle comes into your life, you will reject it." That is why our sages say, practise all that you wish to practise. Whether you wish to pray in temples or perform other rituals, go right ahead, but try to acquire excellence in the knowledge that you are receiving and learning. That is when you will receive the grace and compassion of God, not otherwise.

A farmer first clears the land, removes the thorns and weeds, breaks up the hard earth and makes it soft, removes the stones, prepares beds, and then sows the seeds. You have to handle your life in the same way. You want to sow seeds in the hard earth of your mind and heart. Their present state is not suitable for cultivation. You haven't cleared the earth from within, the thorns are continuing to grow, the rocks and stones are continuing to cause obstructions. You haven't ploughed the earth and you want positive qualities to grow and blossom there. This is like sprinkling seeds on untilled land. The seeds will not sprout, no matter how good or plentiful they are. Until and unless the seeds find the appropriate environment, they will not sprout. They will lie on the surface of the ground for a few days and then dry up. They will not serve any purpose. Therefore, when one enters into spiritual life and wants to advance in it, the first attempt should be to till the inner land, remove the weeds, rocks and thorns, and prepare it for the sowing of positive samskaras. This requires effort. It requires sadhana and sankalpa.

Four stages of life

In the Indian tradition, life is divided into four stages or *ashramas*. In each stage, the individual is required to practise *purushartha*, make an effort, with a specific focus.

In the first stage, *brahmacharya*, one makes the effort to receive *vidya*, education, and prepares to take on responsibilities. The scriptures say: *Janmana jaayate shudrah* – "Every individual is a *shudra*, the lowest class of mindset, when they are born, irrespective of their inherited class"; *Samskaro dwija uchchate* – "With the acquisition of *samskaras*, positive inputs, one becomes twice-born." At birth, the individual is ignorant. The intellect, the senses and the mind are not developed. With education, learning and the input of samskaras, one receives a new birth. Equipped with these, one becomes capable of undertaking the necessary roles of life. Brahmacharya is the stage in which the personality is formed. Raw earth becomes moulded into a form. The brahmacharya stage is not aimed at receiving external education only, but also for learning *sanyam*, the disciplines of life, so that one may develop a balanced mind. Thus, the effort in the brahmacharya stage is aimed at receiving three tools: vidya, samskara and sanyam.

The second ashrama, *grihastha*, is the stage of material fulfilment. In this stage one learns how to enhance *artha*, material prosperity. One works to enhance one's family and wealth, grow in name and fame, advance in one's profession and in society, and acquire status. Thereafter, on retirement, one enters into the third ashrama, *vanaprastha*. This is the stage when the mind can be attached to dharma. Now, one has to fine-tune the mind just as one fine-tunes a radio to bring it to the right station. The process of fine-tuning is the process of understanding and connecting with dharma.

Dharma has been defined in terms of *sadvichara*, appropriate thinking, *sadvyavahara*, appropriate behaviour, and *sadkarma*, appropriate action. The common usage of the word dharma pertains to religion, but dharma has nothing to do with religion; it simply means appropriateness in thoughts, actions and behaviour. It means connecting the thoughts that were connected with *asat*, untruth, with *sat*, truth. Changing the behaviour which was asat into sat. Inspiring with sat the actions that until now were inspired with asat. Worship and prayer are aspects of personal belief and faith, but dharma is a process of change and transformation in life. Therefore, the scriptures say, *Dharayate iti dharmah* – "That which one is able to imbibe in life is dharma."

What must be imbibed are positive qualities. The negative qualities, be it jealousy, lust, anger or hatred, only brings trouble. People say, "Everyone has become so horrible these days. No one is sensitive towards others; everyone is so selfish and cruel." This means that everyone is tired of the negativity they experience, but they don't know how to be free of it.

It is said in the scriptures that there are three major negative qualities: *Kamah, krodhah lobhashcha, dehe tishthanti tasharaah* – "Lust, anger and greed are the thieves that reside within the body." What do these thieves steal? *Jnanaratnopaharaya* – "They steal the jewel of *jnana*, wisdom." They steal *viveka*, the discriminative ability; they steal *buddhi*, the intellect, and they also steal dharma. Thus, the real ritual of dharma is equipping oneself with positive qualities. That is the purpose and aim of dharma, and that is the fine-tuning one needs to undertake in the stage of vanaprastha.

The last ashrama is sannyasa. A sannyasin says, *Bhu san-yastam maya, bhuvah sanyastam maya, svah sanyastam maya*. This means that when one takes sannyasa, the mind is freed from the bondage of sense objects. When the mind becomes free, it is possible to make the effort for *moksha*, liberation.

The ashrama system was prescribed by the rishis so that one could participate efficiently in the world and at the same time become free of its pains and pleasures, so that one could begin the journey towards transcendence and attain freedom from suffering in life. The intellectual view holds that each ashrama of life must be lived for twenty-five years. However, that is not a real-life perspective. Adi Guru Shankaracharya renounced his home at the age of six. We have the examples of our own gurus, Swami Sivananda and Swami Satya-nanda. If they had decided to follow the traditional view, we would not have had the benefit of their presence, love and teachings. The reality is that at any time one is fired by the inspiration to walk in a new direction, one must follow it.

Journey to the unconditioned state

When the inspiration to follow the path of dharma awakens, the first effort required is understanding one's conditioning. There are four basic conditionings in human life: one, craving, desiring or wanting; two, disconnection, shutting off, sleeping, withdrawing; three, insecurity and fear when things change, fear of losing one's comfort zone; four, obtaining pleasure, whether sensual, emotional or mental. These are the four basic conditionings which have also been defined as four basic instincts: *ahara*, the craving for fulfilment, *nidra*, disconnection, *bhaya*, fear, and *maithuna*, sensuality, sexuality and emotional fulfilment. These are the four basic conditionings. All life experiences fall into these four categories. These conditions have to be observed in practical ways and changed through the practices of yoga.

Conditioning is hard to understand. It is difficult to even know that it exists within one, as it adopts patterns of behaviour, thinking, living and acting. Everyone lives according to their conditioning. When it becomes necessary to change it, one tries, but it is difficult, for conditioning becomes a habit. It is like a shape carved from a piece of wood. Once the shape or figure is carved, the wood becomes conditioned. In order to change the conditioning, one has to either destroy the wood or use another piece of material to create another figure. Conditioning is existence; it is how one lives and acts, what one believes in and thinks. It is through conditioning that one can recognize the character and nature of other individuals, as well as the nature of the environment. One lives within the confines of one's conditionings or habits. They become part and parcel of one's expression in life.

Habit does not change until all the conditionings are destroyed. Even the word 'habit' cannot be changed. Remove 'h', 'a bit' remains. Remove 'a', 'bit' remains. Remove 'b', 'it' remains! No matter which character you remove from the word 'habit', 'it' remains all the time. Nevertheless, it is a sadhana of spiritual life. Swami Sivananda says, "Kill this little 'i'.

Die to live. Live the divine life." Killing this little 'i' and dying to live means changing one's conditioning to experience the freeness and luminosity of spirit. The spiritual sadhanas guide one to experience the state of freedom and transcendence through different methods and approaches. Therefore, spiritual life is a journey that every individual undertakes to improve the quality of life. Just as one goes through education in school and college to become a better participant in life and improve its quality, in the same manner spiritual life has to be lived to improve the quality of life.

People ask, "What is the aim of life?" The aim of spiritual life is improving the quality of life, not attaining self-realization. That is not the need. The aim of life has to be realistic. Finding a focus is the aim of life. From the tantric perspective, the aim of life is attainment of Shivahood, which means becoming free from the influences and effects of the world. That is all the aim needs to be: transcending the world and becoming established in higher spiritual consciousness by overcoming the gross material consciousness.

The basic foundation of spiritual life is beginning and strengthening the journey from the conditioned to the unconditioned state of existence. It is strengthening the understanding of how this process can be completed by improving the quality of life. This is the basic thought of tantra, which Shiva explained to Parvati. Just improve the quality of life and you will be free from pain and suffering. You will be free from dissipations and distractions. You will be free from ignorance and involvement in the world, and you will be a realized being. Make the attempt to move from the conditioned to the unconditioned state, from the pashu to the pati state. The human spirit is pashu, the conditioned state of existence, and the divine transcendental spirit is unconditioned, free, radiant, luminous, unbound by maya, unbound by any other effect, totally free. This free state is the state of pati, Godhood, the cosmic spirit or the universal spirit.

29

System of sadhana

To arrive at the unconditioned state of existence, one requires a systematic approach, a process and a method. It cannot be attained in a day. Once a seventy-year-old man came to me and said, "Swamiji, please tell me a sadhana which can give me peace of mind." I asked, "Have you practised anything in the past? Japa, anushthana, vrata, yoga, anything?" He said, "No, but there is an intense desire to do something now to attain peace of mind." I said, "For seventy years you have messed up your life. Now it will take seventy more years to bring it back on track."

It is easy to destroy disciplines, restraints and models, but it is very difficult to establish them. For seventy years that man violated all that is appropriate in life, allowing detrimental thoughts, actions and behaviour to take root in his life, and now he wanted an hour's japa and guru's grace to grant him peace. That is not possible. Even if God appears and offers a boon, it is not possible. Sri Krishna tried to instil sense into Duryodhana, but he replied, *Jaanaami dharmam na cha me pravrittih; jaanaami adharmam na cha me nivrittih* – "I know what is right but I am not inclined towards it; I know what is wrong but I cannot free myself of it." Even when Sri Krishna asked him to follow a dharmic course of action, Duryodhana said, "Sorry, I cannot do it." This means that even if God comes and blesses or guides you, you will not be able to follow what is advised, as what has been destroyed over years cannot be constructed in a day. The process of construction has been given a name by our ancestors: sadhana.

The construction of life is called sadhana. Sadhana is the way through which one can overcome the limitations of the body and the senses, through which one can modify the mental behaviour. It refers to disciplines through which one can regulate one's daily routine.

When Parvati asked Shiva, "What are the methods by which one can acquire the transcendental consciousness?" Shiva replied, "There is a system of acquiring excellence and transcendence. It is known as yoga sadhana." Saying this, he described the process of yoga.

The process of yoga that Shiva described to Parvati originally included asana, pranayama, pratyahara, dharana, dhyana and samadhi: the sixfold path of yoga. When the components of yama and niyama are added to this path, it becomes the eightfold path of yoga or raja yoga. The additions of yama and niyama were made later by Sage Patanjali. Yamas and niyamas were not included by Shiva as there was no need for them at that time. Everybody was living a natural and simple life; there was no stress. The environment and nature gave plenty to live on. Everything was in abundance. People were content and lived according to the laws of dharma; there was righteousness everywhere. Therefore, Shiva did not need to incorporate any other system in this yogic sadhana. In the original yoga known as Pashupata yoga, the sixfold path is followed.

Shiva also included the knowledge of sound vibration or *nada yoga*. He included the use of mantras and japa. He included the processes of hatha yoga and laya yoga. He included the use of mudras and explained to Parvati why all these practices are important to change the conditionings of life.

31

Yoga: science of life

When Shiva spoke of the method of yoga to Parvati, he did not define yoga merely as a compilation of practices, but as a science of life.

Any subject, whether material or philosophical, in order to be recognized as a *vidya*, science, needs to have four parts. Without these, a vidya is not vidya, a science is not science. There are four parts to every philosophy. The first part is known as *charya*, routine. The second part is *vidya*, knowledge or knowing. The third part is *kriya*, application. The fourth part is yoga, which in this context means combining the above three. Yoga is a combination of charya, vidya and kriya. It is a combination of routine, knowledge and application. In another context, it also means to hold in focus the experience of the transcendental existence.

A subject or vidya is complete when it contains all the four parts. Most people come to yoga only for the practice. They learn some asansas, some pranayamas, some practices and feel happy that they are practising yoga. They set aside some time for their practice of yoga. Perhaps they do their asana and pranayama for half an hour in the morning, or practise some meditation or mantra for fifteen minutes at night before going to bed. That is their involvement with the practice. There is no knowledge or concept of the purpose, result or aim of the practice. There is no knowledge of why one needs to practise or when one should not practise. For most, yoga is not a part of their routine or charya either. Human beings are far too worried about time, due to which they cannot make anything a part of their routine. Therefore, yoga remains confined to classroom practice and the approach, understanding and application of yoga do not produce the desired result.

The *Yoga Sutras* state that in order to acquire the desired result from yoga, one must have conviction, and the practice must be regular and unbroken. When the practice is unbroken, it becomes part of one's daily life. When there is conviction and faith in the practice, it becomes part of one's belief structure, mental structure, emotional structure and spiritual structure. When it is practised on a regular basis for a long time, then something can evolve in this life and body. However, people don't have the time to sincerely devote to the practices of yoga. They want to do everything in a rush and get instant results.

Shiva explained to Parvati that a subject which deals with improving the quality of life should be understood in the following manner: one, it must be something that one can apply and practice. Two, it must be something that one believes will lead to one's destination. Three, it must be something which can become a natural part of one's normal activity, and not an imposed condition, practice or idea. Four, it must be something which connects one with a higher purpose in life rather than the mundane and the material. These four aspects constitute vidya.

Two approaches of yoga

Parvati now asked Shiva: "What are the steps one can take to remove suffering in life?" Shiva said: "There are two approaches. One is *bahiranga yoga*, outer yoga, and the other is *antaranga yoga*, inner yoga."

The two approaches can be viewed from different perspectives. Where the practices relate to body, prana and mind, they belong to the bahiranga category. When they relate to the mind and spirit, they are antaranga. As long as one involves the body and the senses, such as in asana practice, it is bahiranga. But when one is working with the mind, such as making an effort to overcome the *shat vikaras* (the six flaws of lust, anger, greed, infatuation, pride and jealousy) it is antaranga. The two approaches can be likened to a tree. That which is visible, the leaves, the trunk, the flowers and fruit, is looked after with bahiranga yoga. That which is invisible, the roots, is looked after by antaranga yoga.

Every practice begins at the bahiranga level and eventually assumes the antaranga state. In any practice, at first one is aware of the method, oneself and the aim of the practice. As long as one is aware of the first two, the practice remains bahiranga. In the course of the practice, the first two drop and one experiences complete absorption in the aim. At that point, it becomes antaranga. Therefore, the effort is bahiranga, the experience is antaranga. In meditation, when one practises visualization, one is at the bahiranga level, but when a vision appears spontaneously it is an antaranga experience, which is a result of having developed the faculty of inner visualization in the first stage. Similarly, the effort to practice asana is bahiranga yoga, but when one is able to maintain the same posture for an extended period, it has become antaranga. In pranayama, modulating inhalation and exhalation is the bahiranga effort, while *kevala kumbhaka*, spontaneous retention, is the antaranga experience.

Bahiranga yoga and antaranga yoga can also be equated with driving a car. As long as one is shifting the first four gears, it is bahiranga yoga, but when goes into cruise mode in the fifth gear on a highway, it is antaranga yoga. In the first situation, one has to be aware of the different driving conditions and shift gears accordingly, but once one has reached the straight highway, one puts the car in gear and cruises effortlessly.

Outer yoga

In Shiva yoga or Pashupata yoga, bahiranga yoga is a collection of disciplines involving the senses, the pranas and the mind. It speaks of six systems which cover six aspects of life: asana, to restrain the senses; pranayama, to awaken the vital energy; pratyahara, to manage the mind; dharana, to

fix the intellect; dhyana, to explore the *chitta*, consciousness; samadhi, to transcend *ahamkara*, ego.

The senses, prana, manas, buddhi, chitta and ahamkara are the six aspects of this physical experience. They are dealt with by the six techniques of asana, pranayama, pratyahara, dharana, dhyana and samadhi.

In Pashupata yoga the body is seen as a container. Just as your bag contains many items, from toiletries to clothes to other items of work and pleasure, this body contains many items. It contains *indriyas*, sense organs, due to which one is able to interact in the world. It contains the life force, *prana shakti*, due to which one is able to live. It contains *manas*, rationality, due to which one is able to interact with different sense objects and the environment. It contains *buddhi*, intelligence, so one knows the appropriate from the inappropriate. It contains *chitta*, impressions and memories which are latent and unknown, but act as the building blocks of life. It contains *ahamkara*, ego or self-identity, which gives one the realization of one's uniqueness in life.

The six practices, limbs or *angas* of yoga – asana, pranayama, pratyahara, dharana, dhyana and samadhi – are given the name 'ghatastha yoga'. *Ghat* means container. Therefore, ghatastha yoga means yoga of the container, yoga of the body, yoga to explore the jewels hidden inside the body.

The Pashupata concept is that of ghatastha. The body is the container in which the gross and subtle qualities and elements are contained, and they have to be explored. The potency inherent in the body has to be exploded. The potency of manas, buddhi, chitta and ahamkara has to be discovered. The potency of prana has to be discovered. The diversions and distractions of the senses have to be restrained. Thus, ghatastha yoga, comprising the six aspects of yoga, is the external or bahiranga yoga in Pashupata yoga.

Transcending shoonyata

After having explored the container of the body, when one has transcended the limitations of the senses and prana, when one has gone beyond the conditionings of manas, buddhi, chitta and ahamkara, one arrives at another state of existence and experience. This state is unconditioned by the external material world and sense objects, yet it is conditioned because the consciousness still exists in a material body.

The conditioned senses and the mind are transcended in ghatastha yoga. Then, in the state of existence where material identification does not exist any more, the consciousness enters into a state of silence, limbo, *shoonyata*. Many later beliefs and thoughts said that coming to this point of shoonyata where everything stops is the goal of life. Even Buddha said, "Come to the point of shoonyata, nothingness. Live in this body, but do not identify with anything. Use the mind, but do not identify with the mind. Use your feelings and emotions, but do not identify with the feelings and emotions. Perform the karmas, but do not identify with the karmas. You are not the doer, nor are you the enjoyer. You are not the experimenter, nor are you the experience. You are nothing; identify with nothingness." That was the teaching of Buddha. Come to the point where everything stops, all motion and activities cease, and you experience inner silence and tranquillity, shoonyata.

In Pashupata yoga, Shiva has developed this concept further, saying: "You have transcended your gross nature, the senses, the pranas and the mind by adhering to the disciplines and practices of bahiranga yoga. Now, at the moment when you enter the realm of shoonyata, nothingness, identify with your transcendental nature, become aware of the transcendental nature, for that is your true essence. That unconditioned and unlimited state is your true nature. Once you identify with that unconditioned and unlimited nature, you will discover that you begin to experience the world in a different way. Everything is energy, everything is vibrant, everything is vibration."

One can realize this harmony of vibration through mantras and yantras. One can awaken the dormant powers of consciousness with the practices of mudras and bandhas which awaken the chakras. One can develop sensitivity to the higher realms of consciousness, where the vibratory field is more powerful and intense, through the practices of nada yoga. This is internal yoga, the antaranga aspect of Pashupata yoga. The techniques of this yoga include mantra and japa, yantras which represent the maps of consciousness, nada yoga which cultivates sensitivity towards vibrations, and mudras and bandhas which regulate the activity of the chakras.

The practices of mudra, bandha, mantra, yantra and nada yoga, along with other sub-subjects, are part of internal yoga in Pashupata yoga. However, it is not only the practices but their application in daily life which allows one to experience their benefits.

Developing a new vritti
One needs to regulate one's life according to the priorities that will help one become a better person, and not according to the whims of the mind. This requires the modification of small conditionings and habits, which is achieved by following charya: adopting, implementing and understanding a

practice, a concept, a yogic thought in one's normal routine. Then, in order to develop vidya or knowledge, *swadhyaya*, learning and studying, is important.

Finally, the mind has to be focused on the essence of the real self. Right now, your mind is focused on material things, on material vrittis. You are intensely aware of your pains and pleasures. You are intensely aware of your desires and needs. You are intensely aware of what you need to do in order to live a so-called happy and healthy life. But you are not aware of your spiritual nature. As has been mentioned, the spiritual nature is not awareness of God; the spiritual nature is improving the quality of life, it is changing one's conditionings, vrittis and habits.

In the yogic tradition it is said that vrittis are modifications of the mind and one is continuously subject to them. One cannot be free from a vritti or eradicate it, but can replace the existing ones with better ones, just as one can replace one's old clothes with a new set of clothes. One can replace the old vrittis with a new set of vrittis which can help one progress and grow in life. Therefore, the vritti which one needs to develop is a balanced vritti. Other vrittis that one experiences in life are not balanced, homogeneous or integrated. An integrated and homogeneous awareness or vritti has to develop, which is called the brahmi vritti. Overcome the five vrittis which cause pain and suffering, pleasure and happiness in life – *pramana*, proof or right knowledge, *viparyaya*, illusory or wrong knowledge, *vikalpa*, doubt, *nidra*, sleep and *smriti*, memory. Go beyond them and cultivate another vritti, which is the brahmi vritti: the positive, the balanced, the integrated, the harmonious, the uplifting. This is what the yogis mean when they say that awareness of a higher reality must dawn in the life of a spiritual aspirant.

Sankalpa shakti
Right now you identify with everything that is external, sensorial, mental and emotional. Who identifies with the spiritual? Nobody. Even sannyasins don't. Everyone is caught up in

their own sensorial, mental and emotional vrittis. Therefore, despite the drive and motivation to develop the spiritual vritti, you are unable to do so.

You spend years trying to awaken the spiritual vritti and not being able to manage your normal vrittis. That is the shortcoming of life. However, this shortcoming has to be rectified through intense effort, through sankalpa shakti, deepening and intensifying the willpower. When this balanced vritti comes into your life, you overcome all the conditionings and limitations, and experience freedom and liberation from suffering, dissipation and distraction.

The purpose of the first yogic teaching was eradication of suffering. However, suffering has to be understood as a natural phenomenon without which life will have no meaning. An adjustment has to be made with suffering so that it is not painful; rather, you are able to consciously accept the change and mould yourself to live according to that change.

Everybody wants to change what is around them to make life easier for themselves, and there is no process of learning. You try to change systems, disciplines, routines and regulations to suit your own needs. Where is the personal discipline? You are not subjecting yourself to austerity and

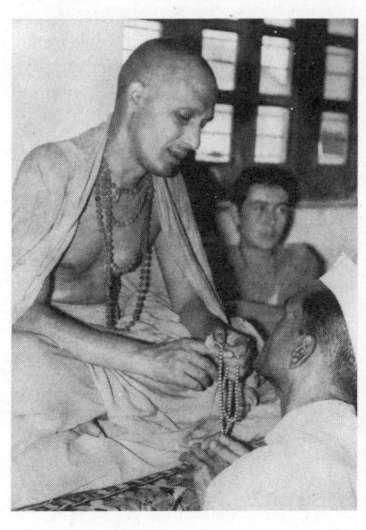

tapasya. You want a teacher who can confirm what you desire. A teacher who does not confirm what you want cannot be your teacher. That is your attitude. It is only an indication that the ability to adjust and adapt is lacking.

In all the shortcomings of life which deviate and divert one from the goal and path, one needs to have *sankalpa shakti*, willpower; *iccha shakti*, motivation, drive and desire, and *kriya shakti*, the ability to implement and perform an action. For any process to mature and fructify, iccha, kriya and sankalpa are the three strengths with which one has to live life. Without iccha, motivation, without sankalpa, will, and without kriya, actualization, nothing can move in life. These are the three strengths that everyone has.

There is a definite lack of sankalpa in everyone's life. A gross example is waking up in the morning. Why is it so difficult for people to wake up before sunrise? There is a big percentage of people in the world who have never seen a sunrise in their lives. It is because the strength of the three shaktis: iccha shakti, kriya shakti and sankalpa shakti, is lacking.

In order to enter the deeper dimensions of yoga, first you have to develop the three shaktis. If you want to read something, you have to use your eyes. If you want to eat something, you have to use your hands. If you want to go somewhere, you have to use your legs. If you want to taste something, you have to use your tongue. In the same manner, if you want to progress in spiritual life, you have to use iccha, sankalpa and kriya. They are the tools and mediums through which the spiritual nature can be explored.

4

Fourfold System of Yoga

In yoga it has been explained that to attain liberation, to evolve and expand the consciousness, all the different layers of personality, all the different koshas, sheaths of human existence, have to be balanced and awakened. Whatever yoga practices are chosen must influence all the levels. That is why yoga is a science and not just a practice. The yoga which has become popular in society emphasizes asana and pranayama, but they are not yoga. They are only aspects of yoga, just as a body is made up of many parts: arms, legs, eyes, ears, lungs, heart, etc. They all have different functions, but they are not called the body. Their integrated form is the body. In the same way, yoga is not asana, pranayama, hatha yoga, raja yoga, or other practices and kriyas. They are all limbs of yoga. Hatha yoga can be described as the arms and legs of yoga, raja yoga as its mind, bhakti yoga as its heart and jnana yoga as its intellect. Therefore, the yoga that our paramguru, Swami Sivananda, and our guru, Swami Satyananda, propagated is not physical, mental or spiritual, but integral.

When Parvati asked Shiva, "Is there a method by which humans can purge their animal nature and once again experience divinity? Is there a method by which one can become free of the traps of maya and experience bhakti?" Shiva replied, "Yes, there is," and went on to describe the systems of yoga. The four principal yogas described by Shiva were

41

mantra yoga, laya yoga, hatha yoga and raja yoga. They are the main constituents of Pashupata yoga.

Shiva's secret

When Shiva began to speak on yoga, he had one condition. He said to Parvati, "I am telling you a secret. Therefore, all animals, birds and beings should leave this forest. I am telling you the secret of life by which human beings can be free from suffering and attain immortality." Saying this, he sent away all the creatures of land, water and air beyond the limits of the forest. He said, "Now I will begin to speak. And once I start I won't stop until I finish, and my eyes will remain closed. Therefore, you will have to keep uttering the *hunkara*, you will have to keep saying 'Yes, yes, yes', so I know that you are listening." Parvati agreed. Shiva assumed his asana and started speaking.

The first teaching was mantra yoga. Thereafter he gave the teachings of laya yoga. Next he taught hatha yoga. While he was speaking on hatha yoga, Parvati fell asleep. Shiva was oblivious to the fact. He was sitting with his eyes closed, totally immersed in the subject, and he went on speaking. When he had finished, he opened his eyes and found Parvati fast asleep. He woke her up and said, "Never mind that you fell asleep, but tell me who went on saying 'Yes, yes, yes'?" Both were puzzled and looked around. They found a small baby fish hiding near the corner of a rock in the stream next to which Shiva and Parvati were sitting. It had listened to the whole discourse. Shiva entered into meditation and realized that while all living beings had evacuated the forest, two eggs had remained – one of a fish and the other of a snake, and during the discourse, both had hatched. While the teachings on hatha yoga were being given, it was the baby fish that was uttering the hunkara. Shiva told Parvati what had happened and she said, "Well, now that he has received your teachings, I accept him as my son." This fish was born as Matsyendranath, who gave the science of hatha yoga to the world.

The second egg had also hatched and the baby snake that had emerged had also hidden behind a rock and listened to

42

Shiva's discourse. Since he had learnt all the secrets of life, he had become immortal. To him Shiva said, "From today you will be known as Ananta, the Shesha Naga. Go to Vishnu, he dwells in water, and offer your services to him by becoming the bed on which he can rest. When the time is right, you will be born upon earth and spread the teachings of this secret science of yoga to human society." Ananta was born as Sage Patanjali and gave the science of raja yoga to the world.

Mantra yoga

Shiva described mantra as *Mananat trayate iti mantrah*, which means that the purpose of mantra is to free the mind from the external attractions and bondages. *Manan* refers to the faculty of thinking and contemplation. By exposure to the world, one reaches a state of obsessive thinking. For example, if someone abuses you, it goes on in your head the whole day long. You can become so caught up in the thought that the entire mind assumes the form of that thought. To free the mind of that whirlpool is the purpose of mantra. *Trayate* means 'frees'. Mantra frees the mind of its tendency to become caught up by the influences of the external world and sense objects. It is the force that can liberate the mind from its obsessions.

After the mind has been freed from its obsessions, the mantra makes one aware of one's subtle body. The subtle body is made up of vibration. Nothing in this world is solid. Even iron, though it appears to be solid, is not. This body, though it appears to be solid, is not. If you could see the body through a microscope, you would be able to see its atoms, and in the middle of every atom you would see a form of energy: the nucleus, which wanders freely in that inner space. It is so subtle that it is perceived to be moving in the centre of the space of an atom. Therefore, if you observe your body carefully, you will not feel its solidity but experience it as space. Within your body you will experience space. Similarly, if you were to look at a piece of iron through a microscope, you would be able to see its atoms and the space within.

Mantras are vibrations and the nuclei of atoms also generate vibration while whirling in space. If you whirl a stick in the air or even your arm, they will make a subtle sound, whether or not you are able to hear it. Science has conducted experiments on this phenomenon. There is a particular instrument which contains sand and if you make any sound before it, a corresponding image will form in the sand. Once during an experiment, the mantra *Om* was chanted before the instrument, and the image that formed was that of the Sri Yantra! Vedanta says that the base sound of creation is *Om* and tantra says the base sound is *Hrim*. *Om* and *Hrim* are complementary. The sound of *Hrim*, which is the mantra of Devi, also produces the image of the Sri Yantra. Thus, just as vibrations produce an effect externally, they also produce an effect within the body.

In kundalini yoga, chakras are depicted as lotuses bearing different numbers of petals, with mantras written on each petal. These petals or representations of chakras are clusters of *nadis*, pathways of prana, that have come together at those locations. At mooladhara, four nadis have clustered together, so its representation is a four-petalled lotus. At other locations, eight, sixteen, thirty-two or two nadis converge. The nadis have been depicted in the form of chakras in kundalini yoga to explain their nature. The mantra that is written on each petal is the seed sound by which that nadi is activated.

Ajna chakra has two mantras, *Ham* and *Ksham*, which indicate that the solar and lunar nadis converge at ajna chakra, and the term *hatha* is derived from these mantras. You can see these mantras on the logo of the Bihar School of Yoga. The

44

mantra *Ham* activates the solar nadi and the mantra *Ksham* activates the lunar nadi.

Mantras are grouped by their vibrations, for example, the mantra *Om Namah Shivaya*. The religiously inclined will say it is a Shiva mantra, as it contains the name of Shiva. Philosophers will say its meaning is "I surrender to Shiva" or "I salute to Shiva". However, from the perspective of yoga, *Om* is the bija mantra of ajna chakra, *Ya* in Shivaya is the bija mantra of anahata chakra, *Va* is the bija mantra of swadhishthana chakra, *Shi* of sahasrara chakra, *Na* of manipura chakra and *Ma* of swadhishthana chakra. Thus, these chakras are activated when the mantra *Om Namah Shivaya* is repeated. This is how mantras are defined in terms of vibration.

Laya yoga

After mantra yoga, Shiva told Parvati about laya yoga. *Laya* means to immerse oneself in the supreme element, to lose one's identity, to become completely absorbed. When creation ends, it becomes one with the supreme force. This is called *pralaya*. When the consciousness of the individual spirit becomes one with the universal consciousness, it is called laya or merger.

Laya yoga is the method by which the individual spirit merges into the supreme spirit. It is a science in which one learns how to deliberately immerse one's consciousness and prana in a state of dhyana in the eternal light and attain liberation. It is the method of awakening the pranas, raising the kundalini, uniting Shiva and Shakti in sahasrara, so one becomes free from the cycle of birth and death.

Laya yoga and kundalini yoga are based on the principle that the supreme energy, which is unmanifest, eternal and endless, assumes different forms when it becomes manifest. Just as when electrical power is transferred from the electricity station to your house, its voltage is altered. At the generating station there is a very high voltage, but to make the electric power useful for household consumption it is taken through different transformers and at every transformer the voltage is lowered. The electricity that you use at home is 220 volts, but that is not the voltage at the generating station. In the same way, when that infinite force manifests in the world, it comes into the body through the chakras and each chakra acts as a transformer. The receiving station is sahasrara chakra at *brahmandhra*, the crown of the head, which has also been called the residence of Shiva.

The different chakras are different transformers through which the energy is controlled and managed. At mooladhara the energy falls asleep, due to which the individual spirit experiences life. When this energy, called kundalini shakti, awakens and wants to once again unite with Shiva, it becomes an upward moving force. It pierces through every chakra and attains Param Shiva in sahasrara. That is the state of laya, complete merger of one's identity, just as a doll made of salt dissolves and loses itself in the sea. One cannot tell where it dissolved, for every drop of the sea contains salt. In the same way, when kundalini shakti awakens and attains Shiva, thoughts of the world come to an end. That energy and God become one. The experience of duality no longer remains; the aspirant becomes established in non-duality, a unified vision is attained. This is called laya yoga.

Hatha yoga

Shiva's next discourse to Parvati was on hatha yoga. The word hatha symbolizes two aspects within the body, *surya shakti*, solar energy, and *chandra shakti*, lunar energy. The solar energy is associated with *prana shakti*, vital energy, and the lunar energy is associated with *chitta shakti*, mental energy. Hatha yoga balances these two energies. That is its purpose. You are alive due to the presence of these two energies within you. Due to prana shakti you experience the vitality in the body and due to chitta shakti you experience the activities of the mind. Thus, hatha yoga is the method to create synchronicity, harmony and balance between body and mind.

Traditionally, hatha yoga begins with the practices of shatkarma, the six practices of physical cleansing. With the help of shatkarmas one can free the body of *vikaras*, dis-

orders. This body is God's gift to you, but you do not use it properly. Rather, you misuse it. When you buy a car, it comes with an instruction manual which contains information about what you need to pay attention to in order to keep the car in good condition. It tells you the optimum volume of air the tyres need, the amount of fluid the brakes and clutch need, the amount of petrol the engine needs, and so on. If you do not pay attention to these things, the car won't run properly for long. The manual also states how often you need to service the car. You need to follow all these instructions so the car may remain in good condition. If it is looked after regularly, then even when something goes wrong it will not take much to repair it. The same rules apply to the body.

The common philosophy followed today – "Eat, drink and be merry" – ruins the body. A healthy body, free from physical disorders, is acquired by practising physical restraint, not by misusing it. Restraint is lacking in people's lives to-day. No restraint is practised in eating or sleeping, activities or thoughts. This spoils the natural habits of the body and mind, resulting in the formation of blocks in the body, which manifest as disease.

Ayurveda discusses three *doshas*, humours, which cause three kinds of disorders in the body. As long as *kapha*, mucus, *pitta*, bile, and *vata*, wind, are in a state of balance, one is healthy. The moment any one of them becomes dominant, the body begins to experience ill health. This indicates that the body requires balance and restraint, the lack of which causes vikaras, disorders. The purpose of hatha yoga is to remove the vikaras and harmonize the body.

The first lesson in shatkarma is neti. Neti removes disorders of the nose, eyes and ears, eases mental tension and provides energy to the brain. The practices of dhauti and basti remove disorders of the digestive system, gas, acidity and mucus, and clean out putrid material from the intestines. In this way, the practices bring about a complete cleansing of the body from the head to the anus.

You have never cleansed your body since you were born. You may have an external bath every day, but you never clean the insides of your body. You have never cleansed the digestive system since eating your first morsel of food and nor have you practised restraint in eating. The speciality of the digestive system is that whenever you eat something, it releases digestive juices. The system does not see that you are eating a peanut or a pizza; the amount of digestive juices released is the same irrespective of what you eat. Therefore, those who keep munching the whole day long overstrain the digestive system and experience acidity, gas and indigestion. This is why hatha yoga emphasizes dietary restraint.

It is said, "Eat your breakfast like a king, eat your lunch like a common man and eat your dinner like a beggar." If such rules are followed, one will never fall sick. One will never experience digestive disorders and remain healthy. By practising dietary restraint and cleansing the body from within, one can free it of all the accumulated dirt and disorders. When the body acquires a state of purity, the pranas are able to flow smoothly.

The first three shatkarmas, neti, dhauti and basti, free *annamaya kosha*, the food body or physical body, of its defects. The other three shatkarmas are kapalabhati, nauli and trataka, which help contain the agitations of the mind and bring it to a point of focus. Trataka controls the dissipations of the mind. Kapalabhati removes mental tensions. Nauli awakens the centre of pranas in the body, manipura chakra. Yoga begins with these practices, not with asana and pranayama. If you study traditional yoga and try to understand its comprehensive philosophy, you will discover that yoga begins with the shatkarmas. Thereafter, the practices of asana, pranayama, mudra and bandha are introduced. They are dynamic practices through which you can relieve the stiffness of the body and prepare it for higher yoga sadhanas.

Hatha yoga is perfected when one has complete control over prana shakti and chitta shakti. Symbolically, it has been stated that prana shakti flows through the right nostril and chitta shakti through the left nostril. The nadi or pranic channel through which prana shakti flows is called *pingala* and the nadi through which chitta shakti flows is called *ida*. When the two are balanced, the flow of a third channel, *sushumna*, is experienced. Hatha yoga is a method of harmonizing the flow of pranas in the body and bringing the mind from a dissipated state to a focused state.

Raja yoga
When the body has been freed of disorders, the pranas have been awakened and chitta has been quietened, the practice of raja yoga begins.

The term 'raja yoga' has been used as the practices included in it have been taken from different yogas and explained in one sequential form. Asana and pranayama belong to hatha yoga, yama and niyama belong to jnana yoga, pratyahara and dharana belong to kundalini yoga, and dhyana and samadhi are attainments of raja yoga itself. Thus, the yoga which amalgamates aspects of different yogas and gives it one form is called *raja yoga*, king of yogas. Being a blend of all yogas, it is the best yoga.

Sage Patanjali used the term *ashtanga yoga*, yoga of eight limbs, for raja yoga. In Pashupata yoga, raja yoga consists of six limbs, while Sage Patanjali included two more limbs: yama and niyama. Yamas and niyamas have been described in other literatures also, particularly in nine of the Yoga Up-anishads.

Sage Patanjali speaks of five yamas and five niyamas; however, the yogic scriptures describe twenty-four yamas and twenty-four niyamas. Sage Patanjali chose five of them and included them in ashtanga yoga. *Satya*, truth, *ahimsa*, non-violence, *aparigraha*, non-possessiveness, *asteya*, honesty, and *brahmacharya*, abstinence, are the five yamas. The five niyamas are *shaucha*, purity, *santosha*, contentment, *tapas*, austerity, *swadhyaya*, self-study, and *ishwara pranidhana*, sur-render to the highest reality.

Yama means a state which can be acquired. Yamas are practices to change the behaviour of the mind, to harmonize it and remove its tamasic qualities, its anarchical behaviour. When the mind is dissipated it is anarchical and manifests negative qualities such as violence and untruth. Yamas are used to change these negative qualities which exist in the mind naturally.

Truth must be practised not just in speech, but in every sphere of life. People say, "You must speak the truth, you must not speak a lie." But I say, you should speak neither truth nor untruth. Truth must be practised; it is not a matter of speech. It must be imbibed. Even the scriptures say, *Satyam bruyat, priyam bruyat; na bruyat apriyam* – "Speak the truth which is pleasant; don't speak the truth which causes pain." Truth is not connected with speech; it is a state of mind. When the mind makes truth its base, it knows the reality and one is able to act and live by truth. Similarly, ahimsa means complete absence of violence. It is not just thinking "I am non-violent";

it means not causing harm to anyone in any way whatsoever. Thus, the yamas are methods to correct and harmonize mental states.

In hatha yoga, the mind was trained to become one-pointed, the body was freed of its disorders and the pranas were awakened. When the mind becomes steady, that is the time to sow positive seeds in it. Satya, ahimsa, asteya, aparigraha and brahmacharya are the five seeds that must be sown in the soil of the mind. These yamas are a process of mental awareness, change and harmony.

Niyamas indicate external disciplines: how to live to perfect yoga, acquire health and peace. The first niyama is shaucha or purity. Purity is necessary not only in one's own life, in the house and family, but also in society. This purification not only relates to sweeping the floor, but continuously cleaning one's mind and environment. It aims to attain a state of purity which is external as well as internal. A continuous effort has to be made to remain clean. If you sweep a room, close the doors and windows, when you open it the next day, you will find a layer of dust there and will need to clean again. You will need to clean it every day. In the same way, you need to clean the mind.

Cleanliness is a natural requirement of life. If the body is not cleaned, it will become diseased. If you are not able to expel the food wastes, you will become constipated, which is a painful condition. To keep the body healthy, it is necessary to also simultaneously expel what is eaten. Accept the nutritional elements from what you take in and expel the poisonous elements. The same principle has to be applied to the mind. The mind consumes many ideas and thoughts, but is not able to expel them. That is why every mind suffers from constipation. Everything that has entered your mind has found a place there. You are unable to apply discrimination to keep what is beneficial and expel what is harmful. In yoga, one makes the effort to clean the mind in the same way that one cleans the body. And just as the body feels relaxed and contented when the stomach is clear, the

51

mind feels contented when the waste has been thrown out of it. Therefore, shaucha also brings santosha, contentment.

Santosha is a state of the mind where *vasanas*, obsessive desires, are removed from the mind. When there is vasana, craving, one remains anxious and keeps trying to fulfil it. Once there is contentment, one is free from anxiety. One still acts, performs karma, but in the form of *purushartha*, necessary effort, not for the fulfilment of vasanas. The other three niyamas are tapasya, swadhyaya and ishwara pranidhana. Together, the five harmonize an individual's external life.

The third stage of raja yoga is asana and pranayama. The asanas of raja yoga are different from the asanas of hatha yoga. In raja yoga, asana has been explained as *Sthiram sukham asanam* – "Asana is that state of the body in which one can remain still and comfortable for a long time." Normally one cannot remain still for even ten minutes, but if one is able to sit still for half an hour in one posture, not only does the body become quiet, but the senses and the mind also become still. When Sage Patanjali discussed asanas, his only purpose was to use them to bring about a state of steadiness for improving one's life, the body as well as the mind. Therefore, his definition does not refer to dynamic asanas, it indicates the asanas used for meditation. Dynamic asanas belong to hatha yoga, while static asanas belong to raja yoga and are used for meditation. These include asanas such as sukhasana, siddhasana, siddha yoni asana, padmasana, etc. By assuming these, one can withdraw the awareness from the external world, become still and experience inner bliss.

Pranayama is defined by Sage Patanjali as the gap between inhalation and exhalation, or the state of retention, *kumbhaka*. Pranayama here means expansion of the range of prana. Prana is not breath. The example of one of Swami Sivananda's disciples, Swami Nadabrahmananda, who had perfected pranayama, is proof of this. When he practised kumbhaka, he would not breathe for over forty minutes. How did he live without breathing? With the help of prana. Once an experiment was conducted upon him at a laboratory in the USA. He was asked to sit in an airtight chamber and it was sealed. In another similar chamber, a monkey was placed and in a third one, a candle was lit. The candle went out after a few minutes, meaning that there was no oxygen there any more, and the monkey fell unconscious after about ten minutes. Swami Nadabrahmananda, who was sitting with his body smeared with wax so he could not breathe even through the pores, was asked to play the tabla. For forty minutes he played the tabla and a coin placed on his head continued to bob up and down. A recording machine was connected to different parts of his body and it recorded a continuous humming sound. Later, Swami Nadabrahmananda explained that it was the sound of the flow of prana.

This indicates that breath and prana are different. When the foetus is in the womb, it does not breathe, but it is alive due to prana. A baby takes its first breath when it is born. A yogi can live merely on prana and not eat at all. Therefore, breath is not prana just as a nut is not protein, but if you require protein you will opt for nuts, as they contain a large measure of protein. In the same way, air and breath are not prana, but air and breath contain prana in large measures.

Therefore, breath is often equated with prana. The existence of prana is a proven fact, and the method to awaken and expand prana is pranayama.

After pranayama is perfected, the practices of kundalini yoga, pratyahara and dharana are taught as the fifth and sixth steps of raja yoga.

Pratyahara is the practice of controlling the agitations of the mind and senses by drawing them in. The mind is agitated because it runs after the world of objects. The senses are agitated because it is their nature to be extroverted. In the *Bhagavad Gita*, Sri Krishna explains to Arjuna that just as a tortoise withdraws its limbs, a yogi withdraws the senses and centres them within. A tortoise withdraws six limbs: four legs, one head and one tail. You also have six limbs: five sense organs and the mind. Withdrawing them inside is known as pratyahara.

When people try to practise dhyana, they fight with the mind to make it one-pointed and focused. The more you fight with the mind, the more likely you are to lose. When I was a boy, Sri Swamiji used to tell me a story. A king had four wild horses. They were beautiful, but wild and untrained. The king declared that anyone who was able to train them would be rewarded generously. Many people came greedy for the reward. Every contender tried to put the bridle and saddle on the horses immediately. The horses were wild and wouldn't oblige. Instead, they would kick, so most people ended up with broken bones. The king became dejected. He lamented, "Such beautiful horses, and there is no one in my entire kingdom who can train them!" He stepped up the reward and declared that half his kingdom would be given to anyone who could tame the horses.

One day, a young man came to the king's court and said, "I would like to try taming your horses." The king said, "Think well. Many have tried, none have been successful." The man said, "Give me a chance. However, I have a condition. I will take the horses with me and bring them back after training them." The king agreed, and the young man went away with the horses.

Months passed, a whole year passed, but the young man did not return. The king thought the horses must have run away after injuring the young man and gave up ever seeing them again. One day, when he was strolling along the palace terrace, he noticed four horses approaching the palace in a perfect line on the royal road, with the young man astride the first horse. He immediately went down. The young man bowed before the king and said, "Here are your horses, my king. They have been trained." The king asked, "How did you achieve this?" The man replied, "I did not do anything. I simply let them be free. When they would run, I would run with them. When they would drink water, I would make my tea. When they would graze on the grass, I would cook my food. When they would sleep, I would also sleep. Slowly, they started recognizing me as the fifth horse. One day, I put my hand on the back of a horse. He flinched, but eventually got used to my touch. Sometime later, I put the bridle on a horse. He did not like it, but got used to it. We became habituated to each other and eventually became friends. I got to know them and trained them on the basis of friendship. That is how today I am able to ride them and stand before you."

After the story, Sri Swamiji asked me, "Tell me, Niranjan, who were these four horses?" I replied, "Swamiji, could they be manas, buddhi, ahamkara and chitta?" He said, "Yes." In this way, he would explain yogic concepts to me.

You have come into this life with four wild horses and you want to ride and control them. That is not possible because you have not trained them. The nature of the mind is like a monkey which has had a shot of alcohol and is bitten by a scorpion. This is the form of manas, buddhi, chitta and ahamkara. If you want to establish control over them, it cannot happen in an instant. You have to first become friends with them. Then you can try to change them. When the mind becomes still, you can ride it. The method of becoming friends with the mind and make it still is pratyahara.

When the state of pratyahara is attained, the mind becomes one-pointed. That is the beginning of dharana. Once

55

the mind becomes one-pointed, it becomes absorbed in its object of focus. It forgets everything else, just as when a lover talking with his beloved forgets the time. One hour feels like a minute to him. If the same person is asked to sit on a hot plate, one minute will seem like an hour to him. Thus, the state of dharana is where the mind is totally absorbed in contemplation and becomes oblivious to the external world. As long as the mind is unable to forget itself or become absorbed, you have to keep practising pratyahara.

When the mind becomes absorbed, the state of dhyana begins. The scriptures say that dhyana has three aspects: the meditator, the method of meditation and the goal of meditation. At the beginning of dhyana, one is aware of oneself, one is aware of the method as well as the goal. When the meditation deepens, awareness of the method disappears; only that of the self and the object remains. As one advances further in dhyana, awareness of the self also finishes; only the object of meditation remains. The final stage of dhyana is where one is completely absorbed in the object of meditation and is oblivious to the self. That is the point from where samadhi begins. Thus, in the sequence of the practices of raja yoga, one learns to control all the subtle states of one's being.

These are the teachings of yoga: mantra yoga, laya yoga, hatha yoga and raja yoga. If they are practised and followed according to the tradition, they release all the conditionings of the human body and mind one by one, so the jiva becomes a vessel capable of holding the transcendental reality and is freed from the cycle of pain and pleasure.

5

Freedom from Suffering

Once a disciple of Lord Buddha asked him why he placed so much emphasis on eliminating suffering and not on spiritual awakening and experiencing the higher force. Buddha asked him to go to everyone present for the satsang that day and ask what they wanted to hear about. The man noted down in his diary everything people said, and returned to Buddha. He said, "Master, you were right. Very few people want to experience the higher force. Most of them want freedom from suffering. They want a solution to their problems; they want their tensions and sorrows to be removed."

This has been the case since time immemorial, not just during the time of Buddha. This is what humankind has always been searching for, and to fulfil this search Shiva imparted the teachings of yoga to Parvati. The purpose of yoga is freedom from suffering, and every individual can attain this. Being free from suffering, one may live as a good householder in the world, as a sannyasin, a karma yogi, a bhakta or a jnana yogi. That is an individual's personal decision.

Watering the roots

What is the meaning of spiritual awakening? You are mesmerized by the material world and thus think of material life as the basis of existence. When materialism becomes the basis of life, the spirit becomes weak. Note this carefully. The body becomes weak when it does not receive food and nutrition.

The mind becomes weak when it does not receive joy. When it undergoes suffering continuously and cannot see a way out, the mind becomes negative, weak and narrow. Similarly, the spirit becomes weak when there is lack of restraint, *sanyam*, in life. Unchecked indulgence and involvement in the material world diminishes the strength of the spirit. Just as the body needs nutrition from food to remain strong, the mind needs joy and the spirit needs sanyam.

Sanyam means following disciplines in life. Once during my early days in the ashram, Sri Swamiji was leaving for a program. There were very few sannyasins in the ashram at that time and all were young. Before travelling, Sri Swamiji always used to give specific responsibilities to everyone. I was six or seven years old, I also went and stood before him and asked, "Swamiji, what is my duty?" He looked at me and said, "You look after the garden." Those of you who have seen the old ashram know how big the garden is – you can measure it in four steps! Nevertheless, when Sri Swamiji said that I had to look after the garden, I was very happy. I thought, "Guruji thinks I am responsible and therefore he has given me a duty!" Every day, I would tend to every plant and tree. I would spend the whole day in the garden, as that was my priority, my duty.

After a week Sri Swamiji returned, and found that all the plants had wilted. He called me and said, "Did you perform your duty?" I replied, "Yes, Swamiji, I looked after the garden every day." He asked, "Did you look after the plants?" I said, "Yes, every day." In fact, I'd become so engrossed in my duty that I'd forgotten everything else. Sri Swamiji asked, "What did you do?" I said, "I would go to the garden every morning and look over every plant, every tree. If there was any insect on any tree trunk, I'd remove it. If there was dust on any leaf, I'd clean it with a cloth. I smelt the flowers and if there was any that did not have fragrance I'd spray perfume on it. I'd shine the fruits with a piece of cloth. I looked after everything." Sri Swamiji asked, "Did you ever water the plants?" I said, "No. Is it necessary to water them? The tree, the leaves, the flowers and the fruits are all above the earth, so why do we need to water the earth?"

What Sri Swamiji said then, I have held in my heart till today. He explained to me, "Look, my son, the soul of a tree is not its trunk, but its roots, and roots are not visible. They remain hidden under the earth. If you provide water at the right time, if you provide nutrition in the form of manure, then the tree will remain strong. If you stop watering the roots, then slowly, in the absence of water, the roots will become weak. The greenery of the tree will fade, the beauty of its flowers will pale, and its fruits will no longer be tasty. By removing insects from the trunk you do not protect the tree. By cleaning the leaves, spraying perfume on flowers and shining the fruits, you do not look after the garden. If you want to look after the garden, you need to do only one thing: water the roots." At that time I listened to all this as

fun and games but today I realize how Sri Swamiji explained a profound subject in such a simple manner. You also know this principle, but you never apply it in your life.

That which is visible, the trunk of the tree, is the body. If there is any surface wound on the body, you will immediately tend to it. The leaves are the thoughts, the fruits are the attainments of life and the flowers are the positive qualities. You spend your entire life scrutinizing these, but you do not pay attention to that which is invisible, the roots. The root of life is the spirit. A tree is strengthened by watering its roots and the spirit is strengthened by practising restraint. The spirit force is awakened by the practice of restraint, and that is the secret of spiritual life.

Nurture the element of the spirit with the help of restraint. Just as happiness will provide nutrition to the mind and food will provide energy to the body, it is necessary to have restraint to awaken the spirit element. Therefore, spiritual awakening begins with sanyam. That is what makes you aware of your inner self.

Expression of positive qualities

When there is spiritual awakening, the negative qualities and faults of life slowly lessen while the positive qualities are enhanced. There are times when an aspirant feels restless. You look at yourself and find that you are full of negative qualities and wonder when you will be free of them, when you will receive divine grace. These thoughts make you anxious and impatient.

Accept those negative qualities. Don't try to chase them away forcefully. Only weeds grow on fallow land, not grass. In the same way, weeds have been growing on the ground of your mind, which you haven't ploughed till today. You have never cleaned it. You haven't cleared out the thorns, stones and weeds, and that is the garden of your life. There is no beauty in it. It is full of lust, anger, greed, aversion, dislike, pride, jealousy. You carry all these things with you all the time, you don't want to let go of them. However, when you realize that they are obstructions to growth and evolution, then there is a desire to remove them and sow the seeds of positive qualities. That is when you become a sadhaka, an aspirant.

A weighing scale has two sides. If you put all the negative qualities of your life on one side and the positive qualities on the other, you will find that the first side is heavier. When people find this to be the case, they try to remove something from the negative side. Instead, go on adding more to the positive side so it becomes heavier. The negative side will then automatically become lighter. When you pay attention to the positive qualities and make room for them in your life, the negative qualities automatically reduce. You don't need to make a forceful effort, for that is a lost fight. It is like fighting a mad dog; you are bound to get bitten. If you insist on fighting it, then be prepared to be bitten and receive sixteen anti-rabies shots thereafter.

Connecting yourself with positivity is spiritual awakening. It is providing an opportunity for your creative potential to develop. If you are able to do this, then you do not even need to pay attention to the negativities.

The dwarf of anger

There is a story in the *Mahabharata*. Once Sri Krishna and the five Pandava brothers went hunting in the forest. By the time they had finished the hunt, the sun had gone down and night was about to fall. They realized that they couldn't return to the kingdom that day and decided to spend the night in the forest. A cave was found and it was agreed that each person would stand guard for two hours while the others slept.

The youngest brother, Sahadeva, was given the first watch. He sat down at the entrance of the cave, holding all his weapons aloft and the others went to sleep inside. After an hour and a half, Sahadeva suddenly noticed a dwarf coming towards him from the forest. "Stop!" said Sahadeva. "Who are you? Where are you going?" The dwarf said, "You can see that I am a tiny dwarf. I want to fight you." Sahadeva thought, "Here is a foot-and-a-half tall dwarf and here I am, a six-footer. I will win with no difficulty at all." Therefore, for the sake of entertainment, he agreed to fight the dwarf. However, this was no ordinary dwarf. He defeated Sahadeva, tied him up with a rope, left him on the ground and went away.

A little later, Nakula woke up. He went out and found Sahadeva missing. He called out to him and a faint voice replied, "I am here." Nakula found him in the state in which the dwarf had left him. "Who did this to you?" he asked. Sahadeva could not bring himself to say that he had lost to a small dwarf, so he replied, "I just felt like tying myself up and resting on the ground." Nakula said, "Okay, go and sleep inside now, I will keep watch." Towards the end of Nakula's two hours, again the dwarf appeared and the same sequence was repeated. Next was Arjuna's turn. He also found Nakula lying on the ground tied up with a rope. On being asked, Nakula also did not say anything. All the brothers faced the same situation, including Bhima and Yudhishthira.

Finally, Krishna came out and found Yudhishthira on the ground. Now, Yudhishthira was one who always spoke the truth. He told Krishna the whole story. "I don't understand what happened," he said. "When my watch was just about to finish, this tiny dwarf appeared from nowhere and said 'I want to wrestle you.' When we started wrestling, something strange happened. The more I fought, the bigger the dwarf became until he was a huge giant and I was like a child before him. He easily caught hold of me, threw me on the ground and tied me up. I am unable to understand what kind of a dwarf he was." Krishna smiled and said, "Never mind. Go and rest. Now that I am awake, I will see to him."

Just as dawn was about to break, Krishna saw the dwarf walking towards him. When the fellow was right before him, Krishna asked, "What brings you here?" The dwarf replied, "The same desire with which I came to your five friends and defeated them. I want to wrestle and fight you." Krishna prepared himself and the two started wrestling. Soon, the dwarf

began to increase in size. Krishna understood the matter. He threw down his weapons, sat down quietly on the ground and said to the dwarf, "You can hit me." At this, the dwarf began to reduce in size. Krishna simply watched him. Finally, when he became tiny, Krishna tied him up in his *peetambari* (Krishna's customary yellow wrap), and sat down.

Soon after, all the brothers woke up and came out of the cave. Seeing Krishna, they asked him, "Did someone come to see you while you stood guard?" Krishna replied, "Ah yes, a tiny dwarf came." The brothers asked, "So what did you do with him?" Krishna said, "I did nothing. Here he is, tied up in my peetambari." In surprise, the Pandavas asked, "What is the meaning of this? When we fought him, he continued to become bigger and you have him tied up in your wrap!" Krishna now told them who the dwarf was. It was anger. He said, "Anger assumed the form of a dwarf and fought you. The more you fought the anger before you, the anger within you also rose. This made the anger confronting you bigger and bigger until it became so huge that it completely overpowered you and tied you to the ground." Yudhishthira said, "The matter has become clear now. You were the only one who recognized him. When you did not express anger in turn, he became so small that he was insignificant."

This story signifies that negative qualities will always exist. If you try to remove them from your life, you will end up in a fight which you are bound to lose, as the more you struggle with negativities the stronger they become. Therefore, simply ignore them and focus on adopting positive qualities, tendencies, actions and behaviours in your life. The negativities will then go away on their own; they will become mute. This is known as spiritual awakening.

Becoming the right container

Once Sri Swamiji was asked, "Is it possible to realize the Self in this life?" He replied, "It is not possible to have darshan of God or Self-realization in this life." The person asked again, "Then what is the use of spiritual methods? What is the use of practising yoga? If these methods cannot give a vision of God to the individual, then why should we practise them?" Sri Swamiji explained, "You have misunderstood the point. You have asked about God and the Self. They are eternal and unlimited. They don't have a beginning or an end. That consciousness is all-pervading; it is omnipresent, omnipotent and omniscient, whereas your mind is limited and narrow. It is a small vessel like a small bowl, whereas the experience of God is like the sea. Can a bowl contain the sea? It cannot. In this narrow mind of yours, can that omnipresent form, that omnipotent element be experienced? That is not possible, as there is no receptivity. The purpose of the spiritual sciences and sadhanas is to enhance the size of the vessel, to enhance receptivity. When the right receptivity is acquired, vision of God is possible. Until then, don't cherish such expectations."

Once a blind man came to me and said, "Swamiji, there is no sight in my eyes. I need help." I asked, "Why do you want to acquire sight?" He said, "I want to see the sun. I have heard that it is very bright. I don't know what brightness is. I have heard that it is a spherical orb and looks like gold. I want to see that." I said, "You want sight to see the sun! That is not your need. Aspire to have sight for that which is your need. Seeing the sun does not need to be your priority; attaining eyesight should your priority." This is what I say to every aspirant. Don't make ishwara darshan, moksha and mukti the priority of your life, as you don't have the vessel which can hold these experiences. Tulsidas says:

Mo sama kauna kutila khala kaami?

Who is as crooked, wicked and lustful as me?

This is true of everyone. Therefore, your priority should be to acquire the vision through which you can recognize and understand the positive aspects of life and bring them into your life. This requires sadhana. This is spiritual awakening, through which the boundaries of the mind are crossed over and eventually you are established in the realm of consciousness. You establish yourself in the awareness, knowledge and realm of consciousness – the consciousness which is all-seeing, all-pervading and all-powerful. Once this consciousness awakens in life, it fills it with goodness, peace, joy and prosperity. At that time no desires remain, even the desire for a vision of God does not remain, for God is always with you.

Footsteps of God
Once there was a bhakta who had worshipped God for many years. God finally appeared before him and said, "Ask for a boon." The bhakta said, "God, I have only one prayer. Always

walk with me." God said, "All right, I will always walk with you. However, I have one condition. I will walk behind you. The sound of my footsteps will tell you that I am there. You must never look back. If you ever do so, you will not find me, I will disappear."

The bhakta agreed, and started walking – crossing mountains, fording streams, traversing dense forests. Sometimes he would hear God's footsteps and sometimes he would not. At times doubt would raise its head as to whether God had kept His word. However, as he was promise-bound, he did not look back.

Once the bhakta was walking past a river and large rocks lay scattered over the sandy riverbank, which had to be crossed. As he continued to climb over the stiff rocks and descend to the ground to walk on the sand, suddenly he spotted only one set of footprints on the sand. He thought, "These are my footprints. Where are God's?" On reflex, he turned around and found God standing there. God said, "You had promised that you would not look behind. Now that you have, I must go." The bhakta said, "God, I have erred, but please tell me one thing. At many places it was the sound of your footsteps that kept me going. However, on the most difficult parts of the path, I did not hear your footsteps. Did you leave me alone at those times? Here also, I see only one set of footprints." God replied, "When the path was easy, I always walked behind you, but when the path became difficult and the climb hard, I always picked you up in my arms. That is why you see only one set of footprints here. You think they are yours. No, they are mine. I carried you over the rocks."

When your thoughts become uplifting, when a natural desire awakens to perform positive actions, then your behaviour also becomes uplifting and positive. This is the state of spiritual awakening in which God is always walking with the aspirant. As far as darshan is concerned, it is an experience of the inner spirit. Surdas, who was a blind saint, is one of India's most renowned poets. He saw visions of Krishna on his mental screen, which he described in his poems. These

66

descriptions are unparalleled in their beauty and vividness. Surdas could clearly see all Krishna's exploits. He would see him sporting, dancing, performing rasa lila; he would see every behaviour, mood and moment of Krishna's life in his inner experience. This means that God's grace is not received through the sense faculty; its vessel is your inner strength and spirit force.

Preparing for grace

To receive grace, you have to prepare yourself. You have to bring yourself to the path of restraint. Imagine that there is a road going towards the east. Now, when you walk towards the east on that road, your back is to the west. When you start

walking towards the west, your back is to the east. The road is one, but you can walk in either direction.

It is the same in spiritual life. In one direction is the world and in the other is God. On one side is the transient and on the other is the eternal. When you walk towards the world, then your back is to God, and when you walk towards God, you leave the world behind you. The two are not in the same direction. The path of the world is called *pravritti marga* and the path of God is called *nivritti marga*. Therefore, understand clearly that your priority in life should be freedom from suffering. Spiritual awakening is a natural outcome of that.

Shiva's teachings to Parvati on yoga were based on these thoughts: freedom from suffering and spiritual awakening. He taught the methods through which a human being can be freed of all the different kinds of suffering: adhibhautic, adhidaivic or adhyatmic. Shiva said that freedom from and adjustment with suffering, both go together. You have to make the effort to be free and at the same time adjust to suffering.

Adjustment to suffering: Adhidaivic suffering is handled by adjusting to it. It is caused by reasons beyond your control; therefore, you must compromise with it. For instance, if the weather becomes cold, you will have to wear warm clothes, you will have to adjust to the cold. If it becomes hot, you will wear fewer clothes. You will adjust to the heat. Just as you have to behave, think and act in a certain way to adjust to the weather, in the same way, to ease the suffering brought about by natural causes, to become free from their effects and pain, you have to adjust with them. If there is an earthquake and your house is wrecked, is there any point in cursing God, your karmas or your fate? There is no point in cursing an event that has already taken place. You have to accept it, reorganize your life accordingly, and continue to make the effort to march on.

Paropkara: Adhibhautic suffering is caused by social or family circumstances. To be free of it, you have to follow the path of *paropkara*, acting for the welfare of others. It is the path where even when someone troubles you, you do not trouble them in turn. A tiger and a goat will sit side by side before one who has perfected paropkara. If there is no feeling of paropkara in your heart, the goat will run far from you and the tiger will attack you.

Paropkara is a force. It is not just lending someone a helping hand. Some people may feel they are performing paropkara when they give a few coins to a beggar, but that is not its true meaning. It is said that if someone is hungry, don't give him grains but teach him how to farm, so he may find the way to satiate his hunger for all times to come. Sri Swamiji used to say, "Don't give charity, for charity is the mother of poverty." If you give charity to someone, they will never stand on their own feet. Instead, provide the means through which a person can be free of the state of poverty. That means is called paropkara. It is the method which provides a way out for others, which provides a learning, fills someone's life with light and gives them the self-confidence that 'Yes, I can.' In this way, paropkara becomes the weapon to deal with adhibhautic suffering.

From bhakti to sayujya: Adhyatmic suffering has been divided into two categories: *adhi*, mental, and *vyadhi*, physical. To be free of them, Shiva gave the teachings of hatha yoga, raja yoga, mantra yoga and laya yoga to Parvati. However, the teachings did not end here. Shiva told Parvati about many other yogas. We have discussed only four: hatha yoga for freeing the body of disorders; raja yoga for management of the mind, purification of behaviour and attainment of one-pointedness; laya yoga, which is the method of total dissolution of identity; mantra yoga, which has a vibrational aspect as well as many other aspects. We have discussed only its vibrational aspect, but a mantra also contains an *ishta*, deity, *vahana*, vehicle, *rishi*, the seer who was its originator, and other attributes. With the help of mantra yoga, one can attain a state of dhyana, which is the same as bhakti yoga.

After having practised the four yogas, the yoga whose shelter you finally need to seek is bhakti yoga. Bhakti yoga has been explained in every philosophy and culture in different ways. In the *Bhagavata Purana* it is said that there are nine forms of bhakti. *Ramacharitamanas* describes a different sequence of ninefold bhakti. *Shandilya Bhakti Sutras* and *Narada Bhakti Sutras* also speak of different forms of bhakti.

It is often said that the nature of the human mind and emotions is essentially impure, as selfishness lies at their core. However, Sri Swamiji says that the real nature of the mind and emotions is like crystal. It does not have any colour of its own. If you place a red cloth under a crystal ball, the crystal will appear red; if you place a black cloth, it will appear black; if you place a white cloth, it will appear white. It is the same with the mind and emotions. They do not have any colour of their own; the colours appear when they associate with an object. When you look at money, the emotion that manifests is greed. When you look at your beloved, the emotion that manifests is passion. When you look at your enemy, the emotion is violence. When you look at someone you revere, the emotion is respect. When you look at a child, the emotion is affection. When you look at the world and become caught up in it, then the emotion that manifests within you is attachment, and when you look at God, contemplate God, the emotion that manifests within you is bhakti.

A change in the direction of emotions is bhakti. When the emotion which is flowing towards the world begins to flow towards God, it is called bhakti. The same emotion is known by different names when it flows towards the world: lust, passion, compassion, affection, greed, pride. However, emotion is emotion. It is the same *tattwa*, element, even if it is called by different names or carries different qualities. The nature of consciousness, the deeper mind, is pure, but it assumes a colour due to the influence of the objects of the world, due to desires. Therefore, as long as external conditions continue to affect the mind, it will not become quiet. Even when an aspirant meditates and attains higher states, arrogance does not dissolve. Even when one experiences a vision of God, arrogance and pride come in the way of that experience. Arrogance can only be dissolved with bhakti.

Shiva says that there are four kinds of bhaktas: *arta*, a devotee who prays for relief from personal calamities or pain; *artharthi*, a devotee who prays to fulfil a personal desire; *jignasu*, who prays for an answer to his spiritual queries, and *jnani*, the wise person who prays for the sake of prayer. "Among these, the jnani bhakta is most dear to me," says Shiva. Such a bhakta does not have any desire; desires belong to the other three categories. For the jnani bhakta, there is only one statement:

Om poornamadh poornamidam poornaat poornamudachate;
Poornasya poornamaadaaya poornamevaa vashishyate.

That is full, this is full. From full, the full is taken, the full has come.
If you remove the full from the full, full alone remains.

The term *jnani bhakta* does not mean one who has studied all the scriptures and literatures. Sri Swamiji says that one who reads and reads becomes a parrot and one who performs seva becomes Hanuman. You have to decide what you want to become. If you want to become a jnani like Hanuman, then follow the path of seva.

There is no jnani like Hanuman and no bhakta like Hanuman. A jnani and a bhakta are the same, not different. The last stage of bhakti is that of jnana. This is where one feels:

Siya Rama maya saba jaga jaani, karanhu pranaam jori
juga paani.

The whole world as Sita-Rama I know; folding my hands to Thee I bow.

When jnana awakens, the whole world becomes filled with God. For such a jnani, the whole world becomes a temple and they live their life as if they were living in a temple – with faith and belief. This is how one finally attains liberation. This is not liberation from karmas, but *sayujya mukti*, freedom attained due to union with the supreme consciousness.

71

Freedom from suffering is known as *karma mukti*, but becoming one with God is known as sayujya mukti. This is attained when you understand and follow the sequence of yoga and finally arrive at the point where the shelter of bhakti is found. With the help of yoga sadhana you enhance your vessel-hood, your receptivity, and then with the help of bhakti sadhana, union with the object of your worship is attained. Now, every form of auspiciousness naturally descends into your life. This is the journey of yoga.

Imprints of Yoga around the Globe

Many thousands of years ago, when people still lived in no-madic communities, yoga had spread throughout the world. This has been proved by evidence of yoga found at prehistoric sites in different parts of the world. The pre-Columbian cultures of South America are an example.

In the mid-seventies, I lived in South America and had the opportunity to visit the ancient tribes that lived there and continue to live there, and to see their practices and discuss their spiritual theories. In this process I found that they had a very strong yogic background. I undertook research and discovered that the pre-Columbian civilizations – the Aztecs, the Mayans, the Incas, the Chibchas – had a very strong yogic and spiritual foundation which was not only theoretical, but also practical.

At San Augustin in Columbia there is an open-air museum, spanning many acres of land. On the life-size statues here, the backs are carved with chakras, the symbols of kundalini yoga. There are other statues in classical yoga postures: the scorpion pose, the headstand, the peacock pose, vajrasana, sukhasana, padmasana. Carbondating has established that these statues are more than seven thousand years old. This proves that the yogic culture was alive in South America in the past and they used the same postures, concepts, ideas and theories as in India.

Similar findings have been made in Scandinavia and in the upper African countries. Egypt had a very strong yogic and spiritual foundation. Evidence of the use of yantras, mandalas and other symbols has been found in Scandinavian countries. This leads us to believe that once upon a time, yoga was a global culture. It was an accepted practice in every tribe, community, culture and civilization.

The carbon dating of the statues dates them to 5000 BC. However, the prevalence of yoga in these civilizations would have to date even further back, as it takes hundreds of years for any philosophy or subject to develop. We believe that the reason the statues were created was because there were no printing presses in those days. Therefore, instead of books, they had to use the statues to present the science. It indicates that they had refined yoga to a very high level, possibly the same level at which we are practising it today. To think of the kundalini, chakras, mantras and symbols which we are using even today requires a certain uniformity and level of excellence in theory and practice. It must have taken a few thousand years for yoga to evolve to that point of perfection.

Therefore, a rough estimate of the time when yoga was prevalent in these countries would be about ten thousand years ago.

Nothing remains constant, however. There are wars, migrations, famines, natural calamities, death and destruction. Thus, in the course of time, the understanding and practice of yoga disappeared from most cultures and civilizations. It survived only in Asia. Over the centuries, Asia also went through many political and ideological changes and many remaining yogic enclaves here were destroyed. Due to divine grace, some people – renunciates and recluses living in isolation – maintained the tradition in India. Yoga was preserved in India in a secret form.

In the last century, after a gap of nearly two thousand years, yoga was again revived by the sannyasins. Prior to that, those who had heard of yoga considered it part of eastern mysticism. They equated it with fakirs lying on beds of nails, doing the rope trick, or sadhus living in isolation high up in the mountains surrounded by snow and ice without any covering on the body. That was the image people had of yoga; it was perceived as something mystical, eastern and possibly pagan.

Even in India, people believed that yoga was something which only renunciates practise to attain God-realization, and that it has nothing to do with society. This belief came about as yoga had become a secret science due to natural, social and political changes. The sannyasins revived yoga, and the first person to speak about yoga to the world was Swami Vivekananda when he travelled to Chicago in 1887.

He spoke only on the theory and did not provide any practice. After him came Paramahamsa Yogananda and Swami Sivananda, who became the inspirers of the yogic renaissance in the world. Gradually, since the 1950s, yoga has become more and more accepted and popular, not as a mystical tradition but as a way of life. Swami Satyananda became the leader of the modern yogic renaissance in the twentieth century and fulfilled the vision of the rishis by spreading the message of yoga from door to door and shore to shore. We are eternally grateful for the timely intervention of the sages for the betterment of our lives, without whom we would not be able to connect with the spirit of peace.